What Can I Grow in the Shade?

What Can I Grow in the Shade?

‹O›‹O›‹O›‹O›‹O›‹O›‹O›

Suzanne Warner Pierot

LIVERIGHT  NEW YORK

PHOTO CREDITS

T. H. Everett—page 22, 28, 32, 37, 41, 44, 46, 65, 66, 68(top), 72(top), 73, 82, 89, 90, 91, 96(top), 103(top), 104(top), 105, 111, 112, 117(bottom), 123, 124(top), 125, 128, 133(bottom), 138(top), 141(bottom), 142, 145(bottom), 151, 153(top), 158(bottom), 161, 162(bottom), 166, 167, 168, 180

G. Kalmbacher—page 64, 70, 72(bottom), 74, 75(bottom), 80, 81, 83, 88, 116, 124 (bottom), 131(bottom), 135, 145(top), 152, 159(bottom), 172(top), 175(bottom), 176, 178(top)

Clarence E. Lewis—page 96(bottom), 101, 121, 122, 129(top), 133(top), 162(top)

Longwood Gardens—page 30, 31, 35, 38, 40, 68(bottom), 95, 97, 100, 102, 103(bottom), 106, 107, 110, 126, 131(top), 132, 134, 136, 138(bottom), 147, 153(bottom), 155, 157, 158(top), 159(top), 170, 172(bottom), 173, 175(top), 177, 178(bottom), 182

A. B. Morse Co.—page 114

Michael Mullally—page 98, 99

New York Botanical Garden—page 20, 21, 23, 24, 25, 27, 29, 34, 39, 42, 43, 45, 48, 49, 52, 54, 58, 67, 71, 77, 78, 109, 130, 143, 160, 163, 179

Geo. W. Park Seed Co.—page 85

Robert J. Pierot, Jr.—page 6, 7, 93

Judy Sugar—page 55, 108, 117(top), 169

United States National Arboretum—page 26, 33, 56, 75(top), 84, 104(bottom), 115, 127, 129(bottom), 139, 140, 141(top), 144, 146, 161, 181

Jacket photo by Gottscho-Schleisner, Inc., in the garden of Freda Foerster, Garden City, Long Island, New York.

Photo of author by Robert J. Pierot, Jr.

Library of Congress Cataloging in Publication Data

Pierot, Suzanne.
    What can I grow in the shade?

    1. Shade-tolerant plants. 2. Gardening in the shade. 3. Shade-tolerant plants—United States. I. Title.
SB434.7.P53 1977   635'.9'54   76–46459
ISBN 0–87140–627–6

Published simultaneously in Canada
by George J. McLeod Limited, Toronto

PRINTED IN THE UNITED STATES OF AMERICA
1 2 3 4 5 6 7 8 9 0

For Elena, Michael, and Stephanie
and
as always, for Jacques

Acknowledgments

I would like to thank the many botanists, arboriculturists and horticulturists who cooperated with me in preparing the chapter devoted to selecting shade-loving plants for every region of the United States. Because climatic conditions differ so greatly in this vast country, I felt advice from the experts in each region would prove most helpful and informative. I contacted the leading botanical gardens, arboreta, public gardens, and horticultural societies across the United States and received enthusiastic help and cooperation from the following (in alphabetical order):

Arboretum of the Barnes Foundation, Pennsylvania; Balboa Park Botanical Gardens, California; Berkshire Garden Center, Massachusetts; Botanic Garden of the Chicago Horticultural Society, Illinois; Botanic Garden of Smith College, Massachusetts; Brookgreen Gardens, A Society for Southeastern Flora and Fauna, South Carolina; Campus Arboretum of Haverford, Pennsylvania; Denver Botanic Gardens, Colorado; Duke University Sarah P. Duke Gardens, North Carolina; Finch Arboretum, Washington; Holmdel Arboretum, New Jersey; Horticultural Society of New York, New York; Longwood Gardens Inc., Pennsylvania; Meadowbrook Farm, Pennsylvania; Matthaei Botanical Gardens, Michigan; Missouri Botanical Garden, Missouri; Morris Arboretum, Pennsylvania; National Academy of Science, Washington, D.C.; New York Botanical Garden, New York; Pennsylvania Horticultural Society's 18th Century Garden, Pennsylvania; State University College of Agriculture, Pennsylvania; Planting Fields Arboretum, New York; Barnwell Memorial Garden and Art Center, Louisiana; Santa Barbara Botanical Garden, California; Strybing Arboretum, California; The B–J's Garden Nursery, Oregon; The John A. Finch Arboretum, Spokane, Washington; University of Alberta Botanic Garden, Edmonton, Alberta, Canada; The Morton Arboretum, Illinois; University of California at Los Angeles Botanical Garden, California; University of Minnesota Landscape Arboretum, Minnesota; University of Washington Arboretum, Washington; Yale University Marsh Gardens, Connecticut.

I would also like to thank Sylvia Dowling who worked with me in the preparation of the copy, Jack Kaufman for his line drawings, and most of all my husband, Jacques Pierot III, not only for editing, but for being so patient and thoughtful during those times when I had little time for anything else except this manuscript.

Suzanne Pierot

New York, 1977

Contents

1 You're Lucky if You Have Shade   11

2 The Biggest Problem in a Shady Garden is not the Shade   13

3 A Woodland Garden—Nature Doesn't Mind Being Copied   18

4 Flowers That Bloom in the Shade—
    Annuals as well as Perennials   69

5 Mother Nature's Own Cosmetic—Ground Covering Plants   102

6 Shrubs—Misunderstood, Misused, Misplaced Treasures   128

7 Vines—The Versatile Ones   168

8 Bulbs—A Blooming Bonanza   174

   Appendix 1 Regional Selection of Shade-loving Plants   195

   Appendix 2 Regional List of Shade-loving Plants   199

   Appendix 3 Where to Buy Shade-loving Plants   209

   Appendix 4 Specialized Plant Societies   213

   Appendix 5 Miscellaneous Suppliers   214

   Index   215

What Can I Grow in the Shade?

1

You're Lucky if You Have Shade

You must have a shady garden or you wouldn't be looking at this book. And chances are you are feeling sorry for yourself because you have a lot of shade. I say you're lucky because you *do* have shade. People who have sunny gardens can't grow the many interesting and truly magnificent plants that are happiest in the shade. It is impossible to give your garden instant shade, but it *is* possible to grow many of the same plants that seem to thrive in the sun in partial shade. You may not get as many flowers, but the flowers you do get last much longer and the colors do not fade as fast. You don't work in the garden with the hot sun beating on your back; it's cooler. And shade brings a sense of tranquility no matter how overwrought you may be.

If you're extraordinarily lucky, you have trees that cause the shade in your garden. Trees are the foundation of a good garden. They add beauty and grace, and they perform for you all year round. If a wall or a building causes the shade in your garden, consider it an ally, not a handicap. Think positively. Stone walls make marvelous backdrops for the star actors in your garden, and unlike trees, they shade your garden only part of the day.

But there are a few tricks you must know if you have a shade garden. Hopefully this book will teach you some of them and make your garden come alive with color and beauty. So count your blessings and be glad you have a shade garden to work in.

SHADE. LET'S GET THAT STRAIGHT RIGHT NOW

This book is not about plants that do well in half-sunshine. It is about plants that will do well in more than half-shade or full shade. Here is the difference. Half-sunshine refers to an area that gets strong light half a day and full sunshine the other half. An area with "more than half-shade" gets strong light all day, filtered sunshine some of the day, and two to three hours of sunshine either in the morning or afternoon. Full shade is known in the gardening world as an area that gets strong light at least thirty percent of the day. Plants will not grow in complete shade. They *must* have light to manufacture chlorophyll. The light can be reflected off a white wall, it can filter through a tree's branches, or come through a screen of wood lattice or other objects. It could also be changing light from the movement of branches—bright sun for one minute and then shade for the next minute—in a never-ending play of light and shadow.

There are many degrees of shade, and no garden in shade need be dull. There are plants with gold or silver foliage, and even some with colored foliage that can brighten those dark places. There are flowers that can bring a blaze of color where color never before appeared. In fact, there is so much that can be done to bring light and life and pure joy to your garden that doing it will be fun, exciting, and full of the most delightful surprises.

Let's start.

2

The Biggest Problem in a Shady Garden is not the Shade

Many people throw up their hands and claim their plants always die in the shade, when in fact it isn't the shade that's causing the plants to die. The soil is the villain. Soil conditions that are associated with shade usually mean not enough *humus,* not enough *water,* and not enough *air.*

EVERY GARDEN NEEDS A SENSE OF HUMUS

Humus is decomposed organic matter, and *absolutely* essential to your soil if plants are to do well in shade. It can be provided by the addition of compost, peat moss, manure (well-rotted or the sterilized version you get at nurseries), leaf mold, decomposed kitchen waste, tea leaves, coffee grounds, and even grass cuttings. Humus lightens the soil, retains water, and eventually becomes part of that soil. Soil under all trees is hard, and under certain trees it is undernourished because the tree roots have been hungrily eating up what nourishment there was. You've got to replenish that soil with humus, and lots of it. If you've never made a compost heap, start. (Directions on page 26). Humus made from compost is your single greatest ally and it is the life blood of a successful shade garden.

Before you begin your shade garden you must know how much humus your soil contains and how much water it retains. Dig a hole the depth of a two-pound coffee can and fill it with water. If the water isn't absorbed by the soil almost immediately it means your soil is either hard-pack clay, without humus, or already too wet. The cure is the same for all.

Dig out all soil to a depth of eighteen to twenty-four inches. (Keep the soil, you're going to need it.) Replace the first six inches with sharp builder's sand (not sea sand, it's too salty), then add about eight to ten inches of humus (compost or peat moss), mixing it with soil, manure, sand, or perlite, until you reach your original level. After you put in your plants, add a mulch or humus. A mulch is any fairly heavy top-dressing applied to the soil. Mulches usually have a two-fold purpose, partly to feed the soil and plants growing in it, and partly to slow down surface evaporation and so conserve moisture in the soil. A secondary purpose of some mulches is to smother weeds.

Of course, if you don't want to do any digging, make raised planting beds contained by redwood planks, railroad ties, brick, or construction blocks. Then all you do is add one-third sand or perlite, one-third soil, and one-third humus over the old soil. If this raised bed is under a tree, you should have an inside edge to the raised bed so that the soil mixture does not come within twenty-four inches of the trunk of the tree, or the tree will strangle it.

Sandy soil must have even more humus and manure mixed with it, because it has almost no humus although it provides almost perfect drainage. Use two-thirds humus to one-third soil and sand to make the soil more receptive for shade plants. Plants do grow well in sandy soil as long as sufficient amounts of humus and manure are added.

If you live on the seashore where seaweed is available, leach out the salt by soaking it in water, then chop up the seaweed and mix it with the soil, and it will eventually become humus. The sandy soil you find in a garden at the seashore usually has had the salt leached out of it by periodic rainfall. But beach sand is full of salt so don't use it unless you are willing to leach out the soil yourself, which is a long and tedious process.

Clay soil is the most difficult of all. It has neither good drainage nor humus, and extra attention must be paid to providing both.

Soil next to walls is usually drier on one side than the other because rain generally doesn't fall straight down. If you plan to grow anything next to a wall, the drier side should have extra amounts of humus worked into the soil.

After you have prepared your soil, step on it as little as possible. Soil with humus in it packs down and becomes impervious to moisture. If your soil is in an area where you must walk, put down steppingstones. Attractive ones can be made from logs cut in six-inch slices like a jelly roll. Soak them overnight in black or clear creosote to prevent rotting. If you do walk on your humus-filled soil by mistake, scratch over it with a hoe or rake.

SOMETIMES IT'S GOOD TO FOOL MOTHER NATURE

Sometimes you have to make your own air and light. The way to do it is with some judicious pruning which is also good for the tree. Pruning does the most good on those trees with deep roots which don't get in the way of your digging. Select branches to prune which will let the most light through. Cut off any limbs growing too near the ground in order to provide more light and give freer air movement. Next to the addition of humus, this is one of the most important things you can do to help plants grow under trees. It won't hurt the tree; it will make it more beautiful. You may need professional help, but it is well worth the expense. A little overall pruning to create filtered light as the branches sway in the breeze is good, but if you don't want to do that much pruning, simply cut branches away to form a hole to allow some sunlight.

THE COMPETITIVE TREE

Trees have strong roots that are forever searching for food and water. Massive walls have been broken by roots in search of food. Giant boulders break in half under the relentless pressure of hungry roots. One need only observe the effect of a tiny acorn growing in the crack of a rock. The roots look hardly able to survive, but suddenly the rock will split and the persistent roots grow and prosper.

In their search for food and water, some trees are more thirsty than others. A willow tree can drink sixty gallons of water in one day. That's why they do so well beside a stream or lake. If you have

Gravel used effectively where grass will not grow.

boggy soil and you don't want to use it for bog-loving plants, by all means plant a willow and watch it sway like a hula dancer when the wind blows.

Which tree you grow under makes a great deal of difference. Elms, maples, beeches, and horse chestnuts have heavy surface roots which not only make digging difficult, but they also grab every bit of food and moisture available. There are two ways to handle this and turn the space under these trees into an asset, instead of a headache. One way is to grow shallow, rooted plants such as moss, which turns into a velvet carpet over bulging roots. Remember though, moss grows in acid soil. Give your soil the litmus test for acidity (see page 29). If it needs it, spread a layer of compost made from oak leaves—one of the most acid of all leaves. If you don't have access to oak leaves, use a mixture of equal parts of superphosphate, ammonium sulphate, and powdered sulphur spread in a thin layer over the ground, then add a layer of compost or peat mixed with a little cottonseed meal.

You can hunt for moss in the woods, but if you don't want to carry back great basket loads of it, try this absolutely insane-sounding way to increase your moss supply. Simply mix a large handful of moss with a cup of buttermilk in a blender, and then pour the mixture over the ground. The moss spores *thrive* in the buttermilk and will multiply rapidly. You can even pour this moss-buttermilk mixture over rocks, making sure you keep the rock moist until the moss takes hold. Do this by placing a cleaner's clear plastic bag over it to retain the moisture. Soon you'll have "antique" rocks.

Another way to transform the area under a shallow, rooted tree into a thing of beauty is to use gravel or white crushed rock. When the roots of the tree are so large and heavy that nothing will grow, spread pea gravel or rock under the tree in a free-form attractive design. Grow plants in tubs or planters in some other part of the garden. Once they're established move them under the tree.

Another spectacular design you can make in an area clogged with heavy roots is to encircle the tree with white gravel and extend it until you reach soil that you can get your shovel into. Around this circle of whiteness, grow an eight inch ring of variegated hosta or bishop's-cap—a lovely solution for a difficult problem.

But take heart—most trees do not have heavy surface roots which make it impossible to dig into the soil. And this book is about those many situations in your garden where the competition is from shade, not roots.

Gravel used with a ring of hosta is an interesting solution.

3

A Woodland Garden– Nature Doesn't Mind Being Copied

A woodland garden can be created wherever there is shade, on slopes or flatland. It does not really matter whether you have a small lot in a suburban area, a tiny spot in the city shaded by a building or wall, or even a minute space between thick shrubbery. A woodland garden, with harmonious groupings of ferns and wild flowers flourishing in their own native habitat, is a superb expression of landscape art. But more than that, it is every man's oasis; a private, cool spot that offers instant rejuvenation to mind and spirit. It is nature's version of a tranquilizer.

Yet, as elaborate as it may look or sound, it is easy for you to create your own oasis. Nature gives us endless possibilities, regardless of the size of the area you have to work with. The success of any woodland garden does not depend on size, but rather on the choice of material and the setting you provide. Limited space is no cause for despair; in fact one becomes more aware of each individual plant in a small garden. An intimacy springs up between you and your plants—each one comes more into focus to reveal its character and personality. Plants have personalities just as you and I do. Ivy is mischievous in its growing habits. Buttercups twinkle. Pansies are always happy. Violets look so eager to please.

Nature's woodlands are full of lovely vignettes, if you narrow your perspective. Next time you walk in the woods and spot a small area that catches your fancy, frame it in your mind's eye and then reproduce it in your own garden. Nature doesn't mind being copied.

A woodland garden always seems to come as a wondrous surprise when I suggest it to those who despair over so much shade in their garden. One never thinks of creating a wild, woodland garden because of the emphasis we have put on cultivated sunny gardens. Yet, how satisfying it can be. And what a variety of rich, green, luxuriant visual pleasures. Bursts of color, often unexpected. Patchworks of berries; yellow, red, and black. A ripple of variegated leaves that move with a gentle breeze. A brook. A waterfall. A pool.

I really do feel sorry for those who have no shade in which to garden. There's little guesswork in a woodland garden. If you want to know how to keep it in good health, just visit one of nature's own woodlands. There's probably more shade in a natural woodland than you have in your own garden, yet flowers, ferns, trees, and shrubs flourish. It's the soil that does it. Woodlands have almost perfect soil. It got that way because there was no wife nagging her husband or children to rake those fallen leaves. Mother nature allows *her* leaves to lie where they fall, languishing there to mix with the soil and become rich black humus, the most nourishing food that soil can have. The next time you walk in the woods, dig down in that rich soil—even a few inches—and watch those pink, juicy worms cavort through it, aerating the soil as they go. This is perfect soil for most wildflowers and ferns. Worms are a clue to the humus in your own garden. If it's without worms, you know it needs more humus. Test for acid soil by giving it the litmus test (see page 29). Oak leaves and pine needles form a leaf mold which is definitely acid in its reaction. Make your leaf mold from these two trees if you can. Another way to make your soil more acid is to sprinkle it with equal parts of superphosphate, ammonium sulphate, powdered sulphur and cottonseed meal, and then cover it with peat moss (see page 29).

If the area you plan for your woodland garden is large, your biggest problem may be keeping it tidy. Nature has a way of reclaiming it if you don't attend to it. Helped by the wind, insects, and birds, millions of wildflower seeds will be scattered. If you have provided a humus-rich soil to their liking, some of the plants, such as wild geraniums and violets, will multiply rapidly, growing where you don't want them.

If you have a brook or a stream, you are fortunate indeed. Your entire garden can be planned around it. If you haven't, don't let that stop you. You can build one yourself, or purchase a small six-foot by four-foot by fifteen-inch fiberglass plant pool with a recirculating pump for under $200 (see suppliers, page 214), and use that as the focal point for your wild garden.

In some shade gardens there are areas that are continually wet. Permanently wet soil is difficult to recondition or drain. A liability, you may think. Not so; not to those of us who thrive on turning liabilities into assets. This permanently wet soil can be the making of a magnificent bog garden. A bog garden nurtures plants which cannot be grown in ordinary soil, and offers you an opportunity for a unique type of gardening. Once again, turn to nature and see the goodies she grows in *her* bog gardens; the feathery royal fern, the graceful interrupted fern, or the lush Virginia chain fern. When one considers the scope of plants available for a shady garden, a bog garden, or a water garden, cultivated sun gardens suddenly seem very ordinary.

If you don't have a natural bog, here's one way to make one. Dig out your soil in the form you want your bog to take. Try not to use straight lines so that the effect will look natural. (Nature doesn't square corners.) Whatever shape you decide upon, remember that it is a trench you're digging and it should be about twenty-four inches in depth. Line your trench, no matter what its shape, with two layers of polyethylene plastic sheeting for extra strength (available at most large hardware or builder's supply stores), holding it down at the edges with soil. The bottom plastic layer should be heavy gauge polyethylene, and the upper layer should be of a medium gauge. The double layer protects the plastic, which does not rot, but which can be punctured by rocks, sticks, or burrowing animals. Most of the soil which has been removed will not be needed in your bog. Use it to make a sloping bank along the bog's edge. If your bog is viewed from one side only, raise the far side so plants can be displayed there more effectively.

Fill the plastic-lined trench with a mixture of humus, leaf mold, sphagnum moss, a little manure, and a little soil. Then fill with water. You will find that the humus will sink as it absorbs the water. Keep adding humus and sphagnum, then water, until the trench is filled to the top with this thick mixture which should have the consistency of heavy oatmeal. Inasmuch as humus and sphagnum retain water, you won't need to refill your bog too often except in very dry weather. If you live in a very rainy area you may need a pipe near the top to drain off surface water. Don't keep the bog mixture too wet. It will become a haven for mosquitoes. The object is to keep the bog filled with thoroughly saturated humus, not humus drowned in water.

The ways you can make your bog attractive, even before you do any planting in it, are numerous. For instance, place different size rocks in a random pattern around its edge. Dig out small pockets in front of and between the rocks to plant non-bog plants which like moist soil such as violets, primroses, lady's-slippers, oconee bells, Dutchman's breeches, hepatica, bloodroot, and showy orchis.

Even though your bog may be an artificial one, you can make it look more like nature's handiwork by placing a five or six foot fallen tree limb at its edge. Try to choose a limb which has many crotches where branches once were, and plant in those crotches. If the limb has a hollowed-out spot where a branch once grew, plant a wild-flower clump or fern there. As the plants take over, you'll be amazed at your own handiwork.

COLLECTING YOUR PLANTS— THE EASY WAY VS THE FUN WAY

The easy way to collect plants is to order plant clumps, tubers, rhizomes, and seeds from wildflower nursery specialists and follow their directions. A list of such nurseries can be found on page oj. Although this method is more costly, plants received from a reliable nursery will be either dormant or root-conditioned. Request that they be sent to you at the best time for planting in your area—late autumn or early spring. If you want seed for your wildflower garden, the best way is the easy way—buy it. Collecting seed in the wild is extremely difficult, except for experts, since it is not only very fine, but must be gathered at just the right moment.

The fun way to collect your wild plants is to go out in the woods and hunt for them. There are certain rules you should follow if you want to give your plants a reasonable chance to live.

First rule:

Take the right kind of equipment with you. You'll need a spade, a short pick, a trowel, newspaper, water, large plastic bags (from the cleaner), and a big basket or cardboard box. You'll need the spade to dig the plants, and the pick as a lever to release them gently from the soil. Wildflowers and ferns like to grow next to rocks where the soil is cool and moist, and their roots are inclined to grow under those rocks. This is when the pick becomes so handy, because in order to lift the plant without tearing the roots, you must lift the rock from its resting place using the pick as a lever.

Of course, it is best to dig a wild plant when it is dormant, but many wild plants literally disappear in that stage. If you can, dig them after blooming but before all the foliage has died. Wet the soil before you dig and keep as large a clump of soil around the roots as possible. More soil means less root damage. Wetting the soil not only makes it easier to dig, but gives the plant additional water to help sustain it through its forthcoming trip. How do you get water in the woods, if there is none nearby? Save your plastic household containers, especially the large ones in which bleach or drinking water are sold, make sure they are thoroughly clean and use them as water jugs.

The trowel is for the smaller plants. You need the newspaper to hold the soil around the roots. If you have to travel any great distance, it's better to moisten the paper before you wrap it around the root clump. The cleaner's plastic bags are simply great for wrapping your newspaper-covered clump and plant, and they help retain the moisture. You'll need the basket or cardboard box to help you carry several plants at a time.

Second rule—remember these cautions:

These are not only cautions, but rules of the game if we are to give our children and their children the simple joy of discovering a beautiful flower in the woods. Many a woodland has disappeared into the jaws of a bulldozer and been transformed into "jewels" of twentieth-century civilization—shopping centers and subdivisions. Progress and growth have threatened the survival of the world's most beautiful and interesting wildflower species. Fortunately, many states now have laws which specify which plants must not be touched. Check your local library or Conservation Commission for the "protected" plants in your area. Don't be the one to hasten their extinction.

Even when you dig plants which are not on the restricted list, keep the future generation in mind anyway and don't clean out the area of any specie. Leave some to propagate themselves. If you come upon only one of a kind, please leave it alone until it has multiplied. Only if there is a colony of a dozen or more should you take any, and then only three or four. Don't be greedy, either. Take only those plants which you have room for in your garden. On the other hand, if you know of an area that is to be bulldozed, run don't walk, and take everything you can to save it from extinction.

When you arrive home with your treasures, don't plant them if the temperature is high. Wait for the cool of late afternoon, then set the plants at the same soil depth as you found them. Firm down the soil with your hands or feet so there will be no air pockets. Water thoroughly. Mulch with pine needles, buckwheat hulls, wood chips, leaf mold, or compost. Then place a basket over the plant to protect it from the wind—even gentle winds. In their weakened condition the plants need a little nursing from you for a few days. You'll be amazed at their ability to revive—if you've treated them with the care and respect they deserve.

DIVIDE AND MULTIPLY

Once your garden is established and you love what you've got, you'll want to know how to encourage more growth. Here's how.

Bulbs or Corms, such as jack-in-the pulpit and trillium:
> After foliage has died, lift plant and separate the little bulbs from its parent and replant them in a depth of four times the diameter of the bulb.

Rhizomes, such as May apple and Solomon's seal:
> Cut each rhizome in the autumn, leaving an upright stem attached to it. Replant by covering with one inch of soil.

Fibrous or Clustered Roots such as oconee bells and violets:
> In late fall or early spring, pull apart your small plants. If clump is large, cut in sections with spade. Make sure there are a few leaves to each section.

Vines or Runners such as foam flower:

In late summer or fall, cut at each side of a rooted node. Replant.

MARK THE SPOT

Many woodland plants die down in the summer and completely disappear. It is important to mark their place carefully so that you don't forget where they were planted and inadvertently work the soil and destroy the plant. Most markers sold in garden supply stores blow away in winter storms because their ends are not long enough to secure firmly in the ground. The writing area on them is not large enough either for all the information I would like to record about my plants.

I make my own markers; for wildflowers, and all my garden plants. They're not only cheaper, they're better. Here's how.

When I am finished with my old plastic bleach or detergent half-gallon or gallon jugs, I cut off the top well below the neck. Then I cut off the bottom.

The top, which has a handle, can be cut in the form of a scoop, or, by taking off the cap, can be used as a funnel for insecticides or poisons. The bottom of the jug makes an excellent plant saucer, and doesn't sweat on tables as clay saucers do. With the middle part of the jug I make markers; some large enough for a plant's common name, botanical name, date of purchase or transplant etc.; and others small enough to be hidden in the plant's foliage. Use a Sanford Sharpie #49 permanent waterproof, smearproof pen for writing directly on the plastic, or use a Dyno marker and stick the embossed tape onto the plastic.

A hole punch, an old screw driver, or a nail heated at its point can be used to make a hole in the plastic. If you want to tie the small marker onto the plant, use something that won't rust, such as plastic ties or twenty-four gauge copper wire. If you want to stand the marker in the ground, use a wire clothes hanger. With a wire cutter, cut off the hook and unbend the hanger to make one long piece of wire. This can be cut into three pieces to make stakes for your large plastic name tags. Bend one end of the wire into a little 'S' hook and hang the tag onto it. The other end goes deep into the ground so it won't blow away.

If you need markers by the hundreds and want something that will be permanent and unobstrusive, buy a cheap, green, all-plastic (not flannel-backed) tablecloth from your local store. Cut it up into little strips one inch wide and eight inches long. On one end make an inch-long horizontal slit.

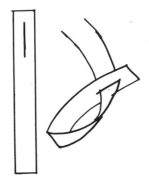

Write all the pertinent details with your Sanford Sharpie pen and loop the plastic strip around the stem of the plant so that the long end goes through the slit. The marker won't blow away, and because the plastic is green, you will hardly notice it.

COMPOST—YOUR OWN FERTILIZER FACTORY

Because so many wild plants require soil which is enriched with compost, you may wish to know how to make it. Compost is the basis of all organic gardening. All the plants in your garden, not just wild plants, will benefit if one to three inches of compost is used each year as a mulch or top dressing. If you consider your compost heap as a living thing, you'll have an easier time building it as well as understanding its function.

J. I. Rodale, the organic gardening expert once wrote,

> In the soft, warm bosom of a decaying compost heap, a transformation from life to death and back again is taking place. Life is leaving the living plants of yesterday, but in their death these leaves and stalks pass on their vitality to the coming generations of future seasons. Compost is more than a fertilizer or a healing agent for the soil's wounds. It is a symbol of continuing . . .

I find it very exciting to make compost. It's like concocting a magic brew. You mix and blend the darndest-looking collection of materials—materials that most people throw away, give away, bury, or burn. You add water and suddenly get a feeling of movement and warmth. Mysterious forces seem to be at work churning, turning, and transforming. Suddenly that dunghill of debris becomes a soft, living, sweet-smelling substance—richly dark humus. Humus is what makes the good earth good.

Where you live has a great deal to do with the kind of compost heap you can make. If you have a small plot of land surrounded by neighbors, you can't have an open heap because it's not very pretty. In that case, make your compost in an enclosed bin or container. The garden stores and catalogs have a variety of sizes and shapes to choose from. You can even use a large garbage can with holes cut in the bottom and sides for drainage. No matter what size you make your heap, you need only know a few simple rules to get it to "heat up" rather than putrify.

Location

Place your compost where it cannot be seen. Put it behind a hedge, bush, or in a bin. Or frame an area with cement blocks. No need to cement them either. If you have to bring in outside material for your compost, locate your pile where those materials can be easily dumped from car or truck.

What to Use

Use dried leaves, grass cuttings, plant wastes, faded flower heads, animal manure, coffee grounds and tea leaves, egg shells, dried blood, sawdust, wood ashes, wood chippings, soil, kitchen waste (garbage); in other words almost anything which is vegetable or mineral matter and will decompose.

How to Use it All

Provide a base for your heap by putting a layer of brush on the ground for ventilation. Compost needs air as well as water to start its brew. Then build your heap in layers. If you can shred your material first, so much the better. Shredding hastens decomposition. There are machines on the market for this, but if you don't have a shredder, you can shred your compost material by running a rotary grass mower back and forth over it. It won't do the perfect shredding job, but it will hasten the decomposition of your compost.

The first layer should be six inches or so of shredded green matter, leaves, dead flower stalks, grass cuttings, crop wastes, etc. Water between each layer so that the compost is moist, but not soggy. Then sprinkle each layer with soil. Don't use too much soil as it will interfere with proper aeration and slow down the process.

The second layer should have two inches of fresh or dried manure. You can use cow, horse, poultry, or sheep manure. It's even a good place to get rid of dog manure if your heap is so arranged that it does not attract dogs. The dried kind of manure you get at the garden store is fine, too.

Repeat the layers—green material and leaves, soil, manure, soil, wetting each layer as you go—until your heap is about five feet high. Finish it off with a sprinkle of ground limestone. Never let your heap get over ten to twelve feet wide as too large a heap is hard to turn.

If your heap is made with the proper shredded ingredients, bacteria and fungi will go to work within twenty-four hours, and their activity will cause the temperature inside of the heap to rise to 140 degrees or more, beginning the process of decomposition. If it doesn't start to heat up, the reason is usually a lack of nitrogen. Add nitrogen supplements such as bone meal, cottonseed meal, more manure, or blood meal. If you have not shredded your material the decomposition process may take six months. After about fourteen days the shredded heap should cool down. This is a good time to add earthworms if they are available to you. Fifty to 100 dug into the pile will wiggle their way through the heap, aerating as they go. Earthworms are tremendous allies of plant growth.

If you don't want to layer your heap, just make sure you get a good mixture—100 pounds of leaves, 100 pounds of grass cuttings, and 100 pounds of fresh or dried manure. Try to use at least two types of raw material. Leaves alone, or grass cuttings alone, are not as good as a mixture of both. If the soil you use is acid, the limestone is a must. And no matter what kind of soil you use, if you add natural mineral fertilizers such as phosphate rock or potash, you'll make your compost very rich indeed!

Don't feel you must use only those materials mentioned above. I suggest them because they are easy to come by on our own home grounds. However, if you want to be creative in your materials for composting, make a few excursions to the lumber yards, meat-packing houses, riding stables, or friendly farms. You can pick up all sorts of organic goodies. At the lumber yard you can get sawdust and wood shavings. At the meat-packing houses, blood. At the riding stable, horse manure, and at the farm, poultry and cow manure. Most people are very generous to gardeners.

Put eggshells into your compost for calcium, nitrogen, and phosphoric acid. Wood ashes are good in the heap unless your soil is highly alkaline. Never use ashes from coal or charcoal as they contain trace elements which can actually prevent or retard plant growth.

Tender Loving Care

Be sure you keep your heap moist. If you have wet each layer you probably won't have to wet it again until the heating process is over. Make the sides of the heap higher than the middle so rain and hose water will seep down through it. Remember—keep moist, but not soggy.

If you've shredded your material before putting it in the compost pile, but haven't layered it, turn twice during the first four days. Otherwise, turn after six weeks. Turning merely means putting all the material from the bottom on top and vice versa. Shredded material is better insulated, gets more air, and maintains moisture more easily. The finished heap should be covered with earth or hay to conserve heat and moisture.

IS MY SOIL ACID?

Many of the wild plants which grow so well in the shade require acid soil. Acidity or alkalinity is measured by a numerical pH scale from 0 to 14. (pH stands for "potential of hydrogen.") pH7 is neutral, anything below that is acid and anything above is alkaline. How can you tell if your soil is acid? You can purchase one of the home soil test kits for a few dollars, or you can make the litmus test for a few cents. To make the litmus test, buy some litmus paper from your local druggist—it's the kind you put on your tongue to see if your body is alkaline or acid. It works just as well on soil. Mix a little dry soil with distilled water. An easy way to get some is to charm it from the man at your local gas station. (He keeps it for batteries.) Lay the litmus paper on the thoroughly wet soil and then compare the color of the paper with the pH color chart on the side of the package of litmus paper. The color tells you how acid or alkaline your soil is.

You can get the United States government to do it for you. It's free (unless you count taxes) and it's the best and most thorough way. First, go around your garden collecting a little soil from here and there. Don't use the top layer of soil, go about six inches deep. Mix it all together and send a cup or two to your local agricultural agent. Look for the address in the telephone book under United States Government, then under Agriculture Dept., County Agricultural Agent. This agent will send you a complete analysis of your soil which covers not only the pH, but soluble salts, calcium, nitrate nitrogen, ammonium nitrogen, phosphorus, and potassium, and will tell you what you should use in it. It's really a fabulous government service.

To make alkaline soil more acid, add two to four pounds of aluminum sulphate or 1 to 1½ pounds of powdered sulphur for each 100 square feet. Powdered sulphur takes much longer to become effective—up to a year.

To make acid soil more alkaline, add ground lime. Depending on the acidity, add from ten to twenty-five pounds per 100 square feet. Don't use hydrated lime because it reacts with nitrogen fertilizer to form ammonia gas which is toxic to plant life.

WILDFLOWERS FOR YOUR WOODLAND GARDEN

The following list of wildflowers was carefully chosen to give a variety of color, shape, and size—a connoisseur's choice—and all do well in the shade. They will either self-sow, or reproduce themselves in order to give an interesting display year after year without too much effort on your part.

The one drawback to using wildflowers is that most of them die in the winter and will leave bare spots in your garden unless you also have evergreen plants alongside them. Some of the wild ferns listed in this book are evergreen, and not only compliment the wildflowers, but stay green all year hiding the dying wildflower foliage.

Baneberry, *Actaea pachypoda, Actaea rubra*

Baneberry grows to two feet high in bushy clumps and has small white flowers from spring to early summer, but it isn't the flowers which make this an interesting plant. In the autumn it has clusters of striking white or red berries. The white berry had a noticeable dark spot at the tip, giving the plant its nickname "Dolls-eyes." Keep your children and pets away from these berries; they are poisonous.

The baneberry with white berries is called *Actaea pachypoda* and will grow in full shade. *Actaea rubra,* with red berries, prefers half-shade. Both grow best in a moist soil rich with humus. Grow baneberry along with ferns. It is about the same height as New York fern and its berries make a colorful accent to the fern.

Bishop's-Cap or Miterwort, *Mitella diphylla*

Bishop's-cap should be grown close together in clumps for a low-growing ground cover. It has a white flower stalk that shoots up from its leaves. But this is not a plant grown for its flowers which are small and saucer-shaped. They are just a little dividend. The real reason for having the plant is its clean-looking, delicate, heart-shaped leaves. Given moist, rich soil, it looks beautiful under trees. Although it prefers to be kept moist, it will tolerate a little dryness.

Fringed Bleeding Heart, *Dicentra eximia*

If you've ever seen cultivated bleeding heart, you will know what this plant looks like since it is a coarser version of the popular garden variety. It also resembles Dutchman's-breeches, but grows from eighteen to twenty-four inches tall and has short-spurred, mauve flowers. It is a delicate, cool-looking plant which is beautiful when grown with ferns, or against a rock background. Wild bleeding heart does not die down as soon after blooming as Dutchman's-breeches does.

It likes an acid soil mixed with rich leaf mold, humus, and sand or crushed rock. It self-sows rather freely, so don't be surprised if it turns up elsewhere in your garden as well.

Bloodroot, *Sanguinaria canadensis*

Bloodroot is a plant dear to the heart of wildflower fanciers. Very early, when almost nothing else is in bloom, it has a single white or pink flower with eight petals about one to two inches across. It got its name from the Indians who discovered that the root had blood-red juice and could be used for dyeing. There is a double form which resembles a miniature peony, but it is rare to find and difficult to purchase.

It should be planted in rich humus in the shade. Don't expect it to take over; it's a slow grower. Use it for an accent of spring color or for part of a wildflower collection. I grew it successfully tucked into pockets of a rock wall where I was able to place a sufficient quantity of rich humus and leaf mold. Although it is a shade-loving plant, bloodroot blooms best in its natural woodland state under deciduous trees where it gets spring sun and summer shade.

Blue Cohosh, *Caulophyllum thalictroides*

Blue cohosh makes a good border plant when used in areas where a large splash of green is required. It is a tall background plant which grows to a height of four feet. Small greenish-yellow flowers appear before the leaves are fully developed, but it is the graceful leaves which make the plant worth putting in your garden. Each stem looks as if it had many leaves, but it actually has only one leaf divided and redivided into segments to give the impression of a multileaved plant. After it has flowered it has a blue "berry" which is attractive. This is not a true berry, however, but a seed with a blue, fleshy outer layer.

The plant needs rich humus with plenty of leaf mold. It can be divided in the fall by cutting the roots into divisions.

Bugbane or Black Snakeroot or Cohosh, *Cimicifuga racemosa*

I am including bugbane in spite of the fact that it likes a little more sun than most wildflowers. You may have a wild garden where some of the plants do get some sun. It is a tall plant—about two to

three feet high—with leafy green foliage from which long spikes of flowers grow. The flowers are usually about one foot long, but I know of a lady who claimed her flowering stalks reached six feet! It gets its common name because the smell of the foliage of some species is said to drive bugs away—hence "bugbane." Its botanical name, *Cimicifuga,* is derived from the same source; *cimex*—a bug, and *fugare* —to flee.

Bugbane must have rich soil full of humus. Test your soil—it should be acid. The plants can be divided in the fall for propagation.

Cardinal Flower (see Chapter 4, page 76)

Dutchman's-Breeches, *Dicentra cucullaria*

Dutchman's-breeches is a charming plant which grows about ten inches tall, and has white, fragrant flowers, a graceful habit of growth, and feathery green leaves. Its delicate flowers hang on their stems looking like little Dutch bloomers hung out on a line to dry in the sun.

Its one disadvantage is that it blooms in the spring and by mid-summer begins to lose its lovely leaves. Once it becomes dormant you will have to mark its place carefully. Use a permanent marker that will not blow away, such as those described on page oo.

This plant needs part shade, and although it likes a rich humus soil, it does not like the acid quality usually associated with leaf mold. Check your soil with litmus paper (see page 29). Put a little into your humus mix if the soil is too acid. Plants can be divided, although they self-seed rather easily. Divide and plant it two to three inches deep any time after it sheds its foliage.

False Lily of the Valley or Canada Mayflower, *Maianthemum canadense*

If you can create an area of moist, rich, acid soil full of humus under a tree where people do not walk, false lily of the valley will make an unusual ground cover for a fully shaded area. It doesn't really look like lily of the valley although there is a family resemblance. It is about six inches high with white furry flowers which eventually become red berries. Its leaves are about one to two inches long and each plant has only two or three leaves. Plants must be massed together if you wish to have a striking effect.

False Solomon's-seal, *Smilacina racemosa*

I don't really like the word "false" attached to any flower name. What it really means is that the plant closely resembles another plant. After all, no flower is false; nothing that grows can be "false."

False Solomon's-seal is very much its own plant and just as interesting as Solomon's seal. The essential difference between them is that false Solomon's-seal has its flowers at the end of its stem, whereas "true" Solomon's seal has its flowers hanging from underneath the stem, much like bleeding heart or Dutchman's-breeches.

It is a graceful plant, about eighteen inches high, and is not, in my opinion, sufficiently showy unless many clumps are grown closely together to create a "massed" effect. One here and one there looks untidy and too much like a weed.

Foam Flower, *Tiarella cordifolia*

If you've ever seen the popular indoor plant "piggyback," you'll know what the leaf of foam flower looks like. Its shade of green is light and warm, its hairy leaf texture is interesting, and the serrated edges of the leaf are attractive. Its leaves lie quite close to the ground, and in the spring it has spikes of white furry flowers. It multiplies easily by putting out runners, and these runners can be cut to make new plants.

It needs rich humus with plenty of leaf mold. Put a little sand into the soil too, so that it gets good drainage. It looks equally beautiful in a wild or formal garden.

Foam Flower

Gentian (see Chapter 4, page 84)

Hepatica, *Hepatica acutiloba, Hepatica americana*

Hepatica is one of the most popular and best known American wildflowers and is an important addition to a naturalized or woodland garden because it tolerates shade so well. In a cultivated garden its delicate beauty may be lost among so many flowers vying for attention since it is only about five inches tall. Its name is derived from the Greek *hepar*, "liver," for which the plant was thought to have curative value in the past.

The advantage of hepatica is that its pretty white, pink, blue, or purple flowers appear very early in the spring, long before any other plant except perhaps skunk cabbage. The flowers are seen before the leaves, but close inspection will reveal unopened leaves at the base of the flowers.

There are two species of hepatica; *H. acutiloba* and *H. americana*. The main difference between them is that *H. acutiloba* has sharp, pointed leaves, while those of *H. americana* are rounded.

It is not a hard plant to grow. It needs rich, acid humus in part shade, but it will grow in dry, rocky soil if acid humus has been added. Mix a liberal amount of sand in with the humus since it needs good drainage. I plant hepatica in stone walls in little pockets of humus—the crack between the stones takes care of the drainage. Clumps can be divided in the fall, although if conditions are right it will sow itself.

Hepatica

Iris Cristata

If you want a carpet of low-growing greenery with little spring flowers that rival an orchid in beauty, you will love iris cristata. It has many other advantages too. It is easy to grow and it transplants without fuss. It spreads rapidly, sometimes too rapidly if your rock garden is small. Its rhizomes hug the ground tightly, forming a carpet. The flowers have blue petals with a dainty, white and yellow crest that looks attractive in miniature arrangements.

Iris cristata does best in part shade with a little filtered sunlight, and should have rich humus with good drainage. I grew mine on a hillside where I had problems with soil erosion every year. A dozen plants, divided the following year into thirty plants, soon covered the whole area and prevented spring rains from washing out the soil.

Jack-in-the-pulpit, *Arisaema triphyllum*

On a list of most gardeners' favorite wildflowers, jack-in-the-pulpit rates a high mark. Its three bright-green leaves, rising from a long stem, are usually taller than the flower which looks like a small

calla lily. It gets its name from the striped green and brown flower whose spadix resembles a man (hence the name "Jack") while the "pulpit" is the sheath which covers it.

There is an extra dividend when the flower forms a bright red cluster of berries in the autumn. Don't try to move this from its wild home unless you dig deeply and take plenty of soil with it. It requires plenty of humus which must be kept moist. I had my best success growing it in a heavily shaded area near a leaky water faucet.

It really has many assets—an elegant posture, an unusual flower, and very colorful berries. Cut and hung upside down until it dries, it makes a handsome addition to dried flower arrangements.

Leopard's-bane (see Chapter 4, page 85)

Lady's-slipper, *Cypripedium acaule*

Lady's-slipper, a member of the orchid family, is one of the treasures of the woodlands. Its pink pouch or slipper-like sac rises from the ground on eight to ten inch stalks to flower between two glossy leaves. Its common name, Lady's-slipper, comes from its bo-

tanical name *Cypripedium*, and refers to sandal (*pedium*) and the island of Cyprus (*Cypripe*). The sandal in this case is supposed to resemble the sandal of Aphrodite, goddess of love and beauty, who was born on the island of Cyprus.

There are several species in varying colors available from wild-flower nurseries (see source list, page 212). I do not suggest that you try to dig these in the woods because the chance that you will be able to keep them alive until the following year is very slim. Many skilled gardeners are able to do this, but it takes a special kind of loving care that comes only from experience. They are too precious to experiment with because of possible extinction. The bulldozers have already taken their toll. Never pick a lady's-slipper. The plant dies when the flower is picked.

In the woods, lady's-slippers grow in sphagnum, as well as in sandy woodland soil under pine and oak trees. In your woodland garden, however, you will have greater success if you plant them in part shade, and in very acid, moist, well-drained soil full of leaf mold and humus. A winter cover of pine needles is helpful.

May Apple, *Podophyllum peltatum*

May apple is one of the best medium-high ground covers for areas where you do not require evergreen plants. The beautiful, shield-shaped leaves grow on stems from twelve to fourteen inches

high. May apple's flower is like an inverted white cup and hangs under the leaves. It eventually becomes a small, edible, yellow fruit about the size of a lemon.

It is beautiful when naturalized in a colony or used as a border, and it is an excellent choice when you need a fast-growing, splashy display of greenery. This advantage can rapidly turn to a disadvantage if you try to use it in a small garden because it can easily take over and crowd out other less aggressive plants.

Showy Orchis, *Orchis spectabilis*

Showy orchis is a colorful addition to a rock or woodland garden. This orchid, with its purple petals and white lips, truly lives up to its name. Its pair of shiny green leaves encircling the single terminal stalk are similar to those of the pink lady's slipper, but the resemblance ends there. Showy orchis has from three to ten flowers on its stalk, each about an inch long.

It likes to grow in part shade, in moist, cool, slightly acid soil with plenty of humus and leaf mold. It can be divided by cutting the root when the plant is dormant if it has one or more buds for each division. If you should be lucky enough to find it in the woods and want to transplant it to your home woodland garden, be sure to take as much soil as possible with the root. Like so many wild orchids it may lie dormant for several years and then suddenly reappear.

Shooting Star (see Chapter 4, page 89)

Solomon's Seal, *Polygonatum biflorum*

Solomon's seal is similar to false Solomon's-seal, but the flowers are arranged differently. On the one-to-three-foot arching stem, tucked under two-inch leaves which alternate up the aerial stem, are creamy half-inch bells. These flowers are not spectacular, but by midsummer when they have matured into blue berries, the effect is interesting when contrasted with the drooping stems.

Both Solomon's seal and false Solomon's-seal should be grown in drifts or colonies, and look particularly graceful when massed together on slopes. They do well in either half, part, or full shade, and prefer a moist, acid soil with plenty of humus, but they are very tolerant of less than perfect conditions.

Some say the plant gets its name from the circular scar left on the underground stem when the flower dies. The scar resembles a wax seal used on documents long ago.

Trillium, *T. grandiflorum, T. ovatum, T. erectum, T. nivale,*
T. rivale,T. undulatum

The Trillium are a large genus of perennial wildflowers, and at least one or two species grow wild in most areas of the United States. They flower long before the leaves appear on the trees in the spring.

They are very useful and charming plants in your wild garden when grown in clumps along with ferns, or in a rock wall niche, since they have flowers in the spring and berries in the fall.

Trillium grow from rhizome-type roots, and it is wise to plant them in an inverted wire basket (the kind used for hanging-plants) so that squirrels or rodents can't get at them. They prefer shady conditions with a moist soil varying from neutral to very acid depending on which species you are growing, but all are happiest in a moist soil with plenty of humus.

The flowers should *not* be picked. Because the blooms grow on such short stems it is necessary to pick the leaves to include the flowers, and without the green leaves there is no way for the root to manufacture the chlorophyll necessary to plant life.

If you are ordering plants, specify that you would like them sent to you in the autumn so that the bud will be ready for blooming the following spring. Established plants can be divided. If you are getting your plants from the woods, transplant them in midsummer after the foliage has ripened. Seeds are readily available from specialists and should be sown in the fall.

Six of the most widely available species are listed below. Consult your wildflower catalog for full listings (see page 212 for wildflower nurseries). All will grow in part shade.

T. grandiflorum is also called the white or snow trillium. Growing wild in the eastern part of the United States, this is one of the most beautiful and easiest to grow. It has a large white flower which turns pink as it matures. It likes slightly acid, moist soil.

T. ovatum grows wild in the western part of the United States, is much like *T. grandiflorum,* and grows under the same conditions. In cultivated conditions both do well on either coast.

T. nivale, also called dwarf trillium, grows naturally from Nebraska to New Jersey, and south to the Carolinas. It has small white flowers and grows best in moist woodland soil which has had a little lime added to reduce the acidity.

T. erectum is also called purple trillium and grows from Manitoba and Nova Scotia to Tennessee. This is the most common trillium, and its color ranges from red to yellow to white, but it is most often a brownish-purple. It has an unpleasant odor and is sometimes called, for obvious reasons, "stinking Benjamin." It grows well in any woodsy moist soil.

T. rivale, also called western snow trillium, is much like *T. nivale* except that it grows wild in California and Oregon. It needs moist woodland soil without the addition of lime.

T. undulatum or painted trillium, is one of the prettiest species and one of the most difficult to grow. It has beautiful white petals with wavy edges and a rose or purple center. It is usually found in pine woods where the soil is very acid, and this is a condition that must be duplicated if the plant is to do well. Use plenty of leaf mold with your humus and cover in the fall with a layer of pine needles if they are available.

Virginia Bluebells, *Mertensia virginica*

Virginia bluebells is a dependable and popular plant. In April and early May it comes out to cheer the waiting world, a little behind the arbutus, the crocus, and the daffodil. It grows to a height of two feet and has clusters of charming flowers which are pinkish when young and blue when older. It has the disadvantage of disap-

pearing into the ground after it has flowered in the spring. Mark its spot carefully and plant an evergreen fern, like Christmas fern, nearby to hide the foliage as it dies back. Virginia bluebells like part shade and do best in moist soil with plenty of humus, compost, or peat.

Violet, *Viola canadensis, Viola pubescens, Viola blanda,*
Viola papilionacea, Viola conspersa

Roses are red, violets are blue . . . maybe so, but only sometimes. There are over fifteen white species. There are more yellow violets in the west than violet ones. The violet color runs from red-purple to lavender, but it is mostly blue. There are over seventy-five species in the United States, and twenty-five in California alone.

The shape of the flowers in most of the species is the same—a pansy in miniature—but the shape of the leaf varies greatly, from feathery foliage to a leaf shaped like an arrow, a lance, a heart, or a circle.

You can pick all you want of the lovely little flowers without destroying their seed heads because in most (not all) species the seeds do not come from the showy flowers which you recognize as violets, but from tiny "flowers" which develop underground and surface only when they are ready to sow their seed. Violets are capable of shooting their small seed capsules as far as nine feet. You won't have just one wild violet in your garden, you'll have hundreds. They

are easy to transplant. I just dig them up and move them wherever I want them.

The young leaves are delicious in salads and make an attractive conversation piece. In France the flowers are candied for confectionary purposes.

Most violets prefer to grow in part shade in rich, moist soil filled with leaf mold, compost, or peat moss. But it is a very adaptable plant and I find it does as well in my vegetable garden in full sun as in the shady, wild garden. If you are searching for something that will thrive under your maples and beeches despite their big surface roots, dig a pocket a few inches deep between the roots, fill with compost, soil, and leaf mold, and plant violets. They will do well as long as you keep the soil moist.

BIG PLANTS

V. canadensis, called canada violet, is probably the most showy violet of them all. It is found from Canada to Arizona. It grows twelve to eighteen inches high, and has beautiful white flowers with a yellow center and heart-shaped leaves.

V. pubescens, downy yellow violet, is tall with bright-yellow flowers and heart-shaped leaves softly covered with down. It grows from Canada south to the Carolinas, and west to Mississippi.

UNUSUALLY FRAGRANT

V. blanda, called sweet white violet, is a dainty little plant only three to five inches high, with a very fragrant white flower. Its leaves are rounded.

FAST-SPREADING

V. papilionaceae or meadow blue violet, has blue flowers which come from four to six inch little clumps. It likes very moist conditions. This common violet is found everywhere from Maine to Wyoming.

PROFUSELY FLOWERING

V. conspersa, called dog violet, is very generous with its purple flowers which look charming in your garden, but are not especially good for picking since their stems are short. The plant is nicely shaped with round to heart-shaped leaves. It's found from Canada south to Georgia.

Wild Geranium, *Geranium maculatum*

Wild geranium is a dainty, free-flowering plant about eighteen to twenty-four inches high with a pretty pink flower and delicate leaves which one might be tempted to pick. Don't. The flowers wilt within the hour. I shall never forget the look of disappointment on my daughter Elena's face when she came from a walk with our dog, with a pretty bunch of wild geranium for me. She arranged them attractively in a vase, and almost before she had finished they were drooping.

They look best when grown in a bunch. It does not take too long to get a rather large colony of them since they self-seed very easily. In fact, if you're not careful they will take over your garden. They do best in part shade and in a rich moist soil. They grow from Canada south to the Carolinas, and west to Kansas.

Wild Ginger, *Asarum canadense*

Wild ginger is one of the best plants for use as a ground cover in either a wild or cultivated garden where you want a low-growing, tidy look with rich, green color. The plant has three-inch, heart-shaped leaves which grow in pairs covering an insignificant little flower. It is an important plant in your wild collection because of those beautiful leaves. The roots can be eaten, and in the spring they taste like true ginger. As it gets older, the root becomes bitter. The Indians ate the root to settle their stomachs.

It must have a rich, moist, slightly acid soil with plenty of humus. It grows from Canada to North Carolina, and west to the Mississippi.

WOODLAND PLANTS FOR BOG CONDITIONS

Bluebeads, *Clintonia borealis*

Bluebeads is an attractive plant particularly when grown in colonies. But it is not one to own if you want your garden to take care of itself. It is very fussy about its conditions, and given shady, damp, humus-rich soil, it thrives beautifully. It will take almost full shade. Bog conditions are excellent for it—even an artificial bog (directions for making one on page 20).

The plant has two or three broad leaves which look a little like lily-of-the valley leaves, and from their center comes a single seven-inch stalk bearing three to six charming bell-like chartreuse flowers. In the autumn it has a dark blue berry where each flower has been.

The plant may be divided by cutting the rhizomes in the spring or fall. If the plant is happy it will grow like a weed—if it isn't, you'll have trouble keeping it alive. The secret is *very* damp, rich humus and plenty of shade. But if you can give it the right conditions you'll be very happy with your choice.

Bluebeads

Indian Cucumber Root, *Medeola virginiana*

Indian cucumber root will do well in full shade if it is grown in the bog conditions it likes. Its foliage is most interesting. Its base has a whorl of five to nine leaves. A twelve to eighteen inch stem

rises from the leaves, and another whorl of three leaves is found at the summit. The flower, which hangs under the top whorl of leaves, is small and greenish-yellow; however the beauty of the plant is not the flower, but the shape and arrangement of its leaves.

Give it plenty of leaf mold and humus. If you have a tree which provides deep shade, make an artificial bog under it and plant Indian cucumber root. Incidentally, the white root is succulent and edible, and tastes a little like cucumber.

Skunk Cabbage, *Symplocarpus foetidus*

You know spring is definitely on the way when the first skunk cabbage appears. The odor of this plant when stepped upon, is descriptive of its unfortunate name. It has bright, apple-green leaves which start life as a tightly furled cone and open to become one to two feet long and ten to twelve inches wide.

Why it flowers so easily, and often in snow, is a fascinating example of nature's desire to recreate its marvelous gifts. The flowers are formed underground in the autumn, and generate such heat by their rapid growth that they thaw the soil in their eagerness to appear. It has a small flower with an interesting purple and brown hood over it which, if hung upside down and dried, makes an interesting accent in a dried flower arrangement. However it is the leaves which make it a showy garden plant.

It *must* grow in a shady bog, and because its leaves become quite large, it needs a good deal of room. I used to live in the woods where, to my dismay, the river overflowed its banks every year. I never planted skunk cabbage, but each time the flood receded, I was rewarded for its damage by the sudden appearance of this interesting plant with its handsome green leaves.

WOODLAND PLANTS THAT ARE EVERGREEN

Creeping Snowberry, *Gaultheria hispidula*

Creeping snowberry is a dainty ground cover for an area where you want a small, flat, tidy look. Unlike so many of the plants found in the wild, it is evergreen. It has dark, avocado-green leaves, tiny, white bell-shaped flowers in the spring, and lovely white berries thereafter. The leaves are delicious with sugar and cream, and preserves can be made from them. It is a useful plant grown in pockets of a stone wall.

It requires a cool, rich, humus acid soil to which leaf mold mulch should be added each year. The plant layers itself and can be propagated by cutting wherever it has rooted itself along its slender stems.

Galax, *Galax aphylla*

You may have seen the leaves of galax in florists, without knowing what they were. They are stiff, shining, slightly heart-shaped, and about five inches wide. They are used in nosegays, wrapped around bridesmaids' bouquets, or tucked in with little bunches of violets.

Wherever a beautiful patch of green is desired in full shade, galax can be used, but it needs a rich, moist, acid soil with good drainage. In the spring it has white flower spikes as an extra bonus. I used galax as an edging for my woodland path. So many wild plants disappear in the winter, but galax, which turns a little red when exposed to the cold, remains as a lovely guide to a winding path.

Oconee Bells, *Shortia galacifolia*

Tucked into a rock garden, or peeking out from a pocket in a stone wall, oconee bells is an attractive little plant. It has white or pink flowers, and evergreen leaves which turn red in the autumn. Many years ago a poll of garden club women revealed that this was their favorite spring plant.

It grows in clumps three to six inches high from creeping rootstocks. Its dainty flowers bloom in the spring and are about one inch wide. Each plant has from eight to ten flowers. It may be an old wives tale, but I have heard that while rabbits sometimes eat the foliage of oconee bells (sometimes called shortia), they won't touch them when grown in the shade of a maidenhair fern. Since I've never had rabbits in my garden I have not personally verified this.

The plant requires cool, rich humus which is acid, moist, and

very well-drained. Mix plenty of sand with your leaf mold or compost. It is almost impossible to grow from seed, and difficult to propagate when dug from the native woodlands. It is best to begin with a plant purchased from a wildflower nursery specialist (see page 212), and when the plant is big enough, divide the clump shortly after it has bloomed.

Partridgeberry, *Mitchella repens*

Partridgeberry is the dainty plant with the little red berries and shiny round leaves so often seen in terrariums given as Christmas gifts. For it to do well in a cultivated garden it must have woodland conditions—cool, moist, acid soil, rich in humus and leaf mold. Plant it near your wildflowers and ferns which like the same conditions. Partridgeberry is evergreen, lies close to the ground, has tiny-quarter-inch whitish flowers in the spring, and sometimes has variegated leaves.

Partridgeberry

Wintergreen, *Gaultheria procumbens*

If you live on the east coast and have a woodland garden, wintergreen is a charming native ground cover. But it does require moist, acid soil to which sand has been added.

It grows about three inches high, with little leaves from one-

half to one inch long, and has white flowers in the spring and red edible berries in the fall. The extract "wintergreen" is made from this plant. It looks interesting tucked between rocks, and it is one of the plants recommended by the Audubon Society for attracting birds to your garden.

WOODLAND SHRUBS

Azaleas (see Chapter 6, page 155)
Oakleaf Hydrangea (see Chapter 6, page 138)
Rhododendron (see Chapter 6, page 155)
Spicebush (see Chapter 6, page 140)

WOODLAND FERNS

It was Thoreau who said " . . . nature made ferns for pure leaves." Indeed she did. The great beauty of their leaves, their variety of graceful forms, and their myriad shades of green, make ferns vastly interesting plants. They are always spectacular whether in a woodland or cultivated garden. Tall ones can be used as a background for a formal flower garden. Evergreen ferns are perfect with wildflowers since they provide greenery after the wildflowers disappear. Not all ferns like acid woodland soil, so carefully select those you plant with wildflowers.

Unlike most plants which flower first and then produce seeds, ferns reproduce from spores on fertile leaves. Ferns have two types of leaves, sterile and fertile. The fertile ones usually have the little spores on the underside of their leaf, but the sterile leaves have none. Sometimes, as in the case of the cinnamon fern, the fertile leaf doesn't resemble a leaf at all, but looks like a long narrow tassle of tiny, cinnamon-colored beads. Regardless of its size or shape, a leaf is fertile when it bears spores capable of producing a new generation. Usually the sterile leaf is the more beautiful.

The following selection of ferns was chosen to fit every situation—tall, short, evergreen, deciduous, acid-loving, lime-loving, wanting moist soil or bog conditions, part shade or full shade. The satisfying thing about ferns is that no matter which you choose, you'll have an effective display. And with each passing year they will not only increase in size and become even more beautiful, but they'll multiply too, adding additional plants to your garden.

They all *prefer* shade, but you'll find some on the list that can take sun.

Evergreen Ferns

Christmas Fern, *Polystichum acrostichoides*

Christmas fern is the single most important plant in my woodland garden and perhaps even in my whole shade garden. It is beautiful, but that's an understatement. It is a strong, durable grower. Its leaves, up to thirty inches long and five inches wide, are truly evergreen, even during the cold winter months. It is spectacular when used alone, as an edging plant, or massed in a bed. Its evergreen leaves cover the dying foliage of other spring plants such as Dutchman's breeches whose leaves die back after flowering. It transplants easily and it is excellent in preventing soil erosion when planted on banks, since the older prostrate leaves form thick, soil-retaining mats. It is called Christmas fern for two reasons. It is green at Christmas, and each leaflet on the leaf has a little lobe which resembles Santa Claus' boot.

If given a humus-rich acid soil, it will grow well in almost any

degree of shade, and is also tolerant of considerable sunlight. It is found in the wild from Canada south to Arkansas, and west to the Mississippi.

Common Polypody, *Polypodium vulgare*

Common polypody resembles most people's idea of a house fern. It has leathery leaves ten inches long and two inches wide. It is evergreen even in our coldest areas, and its rhizomes form a mat on the soil which makes it a useful plant in preventing soil erosion. In its native woodlands it sometimes grows right on top of boulders, giving it the name rock-cap fern in some areas.

It grows best in acid, humus-rich woodland soil in partial shade. It will tolerate a little dryness, but prefers to be kept moist. It is found from Canada south to Arkansas.

Ebony Spleenwort, *Asplenium platyneuron*

Although some of the fronds of the ebony spleenwort may be up to eighteen inches long and one to two inches wide, others may be only five or six inches long, thus giving it the appearance of a lit-

Common Polypody

Ebony Spleenwort

tle plant. Because it is evergreen, it is useful in a rock garden with limited space, where a little accent of green contrasts beautifully between the rocks.

In the wild, this fern is found in limestone ledges and in red sandy soil, and the same conditions must be imitated if it is to do well in your garden. Plant it between limestone or sandstone rocks, or add ground limestone, crushed oyster, or egg shells for alkalinity. It is found from Maine south to Georgia, west to Texas, and occasionally as far west as Colorado.

Marginal Shield Fern, *Dryopteris marginalis*

A graceful, dark-blue-green fern with leaves up to eighteen inches long and six to seven inches wide, marginal shield fern is one of the Big Three of your woodland garden because it is both evergreen and large. It does not spread. It gets its name from the shape and location of its sori (the organ on a fern which produces spores) which line the edges of the leaflets.

Plant it in rich compost or leaf mold and keep the soil moist. It will grow in full shade to filtered sun. It is found in its native habitat from Canada south to Georgia, and west to Northern Texas.

Ferns Which Spread Rapidly

Broad Beech Fern, *Thelypteris hexagonoptera*

The fronds of the broad beech fern are so broad and tapering they appear to be almost triangular. They are an apple-green color and grow about twelve to eighteen inches tall, and they have a neat, tidy look about them. The plant's shallow rhizomes spread rapidly so that in a short time it provides a dense area of green.

The plant does best in acid soil with plenty of peat, leaf mold, or compost. It should be kept moist. It is found from southeastern Canada, south to Georgia and west to Texas.

Hay-scented Fern, *Dennstaedtia punctilobula*

Hay-scented fern, when crushed, smells a little like freshly cut hay. It is sometimes described as a pest because it is such a strong and pervasive grower. But it is a feathery, two-foot, chartreuse fern with full, graceful leaves. Because of the dense matting of its underground rhizomes it is an excellent choice as a hillside ground cover to prevent erosion.

It is a very cooperative plant—growing equally well in full sun or full shade. It is equally tolerant of wet or dry conditions. It does best in slightly acid woodland soil. It is found from Canada south to Georgia, and west to Tennessee.

Long Beech Fern, *Thelypteris Phegopteris*

The long beech fern is similar to the broad beech fern. There are differences important to those studying ferns, but for the average gardener it is sufficient to note that it has the same triangular shape, but is smaller and rarely grows taller than ten to fifteen inches. It is a delicate shade of green.

It is a fast grower and spreads rapidly, and is ideal as a summer ground cover that will reappear year after year. It is such a rampant grower that many gardeners sink a metal or plastic barrier into the ground to prevent the pervasive rhizomes from "taking over" the area. It is found from eastern Canada south to Tennessee, and in the Pacific Northwest.

Ferns Which Grow Very Tall

Cinnamon Fern, *Osmunda cinnamomea*

Cinnamon fern leaves are from two to four feet tall, have a waxy green color, and are very graceful. The fern is easy to identify because its fertile and sterile leaves are unique. The sterile leaves look like typical fern leaves. The fertile ones don't resemble a leaf at all, but a narrow tassle of tiny cinnamon-colored beads. In early summer when the beautiful green sterile leaves appear, the plant is still easy to identify because the withered fertile leaf (sometimes called a "cinnamon stick") can be found at the base of the plant. Once the "cinnamon stick" disappears, the plant is difficult to identify.

Cinnamon fern should be grown in wet, acid soil enriched with plenty of leaf mold, compost, or peat. If it grows in your woods, dig

some clumps for your home garden; it is excellent not only for a woodland garden, but as a background for annuals and perennials. It is found throughout the northeast, south to Georgia, and west to New Mexico.

Goldie's Fern, *Dryopteris goldiana*

I once saw leaves of Goldie's fern sixty inches tall, although the norm is about forty to forty-five inches in length and fourteen inches in width. It is ideal for those areas where you want a large fern that does not multiply. It is sometimes called giant wood fern. Goldie's fern is not gold. It is deep green, and gets its name from the American botanist John Goldie (1793–1886).

It requires rich acid soil with plenty of compost or leaf mold, and should be kept cool and moist at all times. When planting, place large stones near the roots to help keep them cool. Mist during spells of hot weather. Goldie's fern is found from Canada south to Tennessee, and west to Iowa.

Ostrich Fern, *Matteuccia struthiopteris pensylvanica*

The ostrich fern is tall and elegant with richly dark green leaves which, under ideal conditions, reach five feet. Even in an average garden, a height of four feet is not unusual. The secret is water; the fern loves it.

In its wild state it is found along the edges of cool streams and in marshy areas. The closer you can duplicate these conditions, the taller and more lush your fern will be. It multiplies by putting out dense underground runners which spread everywhere, so choose your planting area very carefully. It is an excellent plant to use as a backdrop for a perennial or annual garden.

Ostrich fern grows wild from Alaska to Newfoundland and down the east coast, south to Virginia, and west to Missouri.

Ferns Which Must be Kept Moist

Bulblet Bladder Fern, *Cystopteris bulbifera*

The bulblet bladder fern has narrow, delicate leaves from two to three feet long, and looks lovely in a rock garden. It differs from most of the ferns discussed in this book because it prefers a soil which is neutral to slightly alkaline. In the woods it is generally found growing in the crack of limestone rocks. When you take it from the woods for your garden, bring some of the limestone rock back with you to incorporate into the soil. Use the litmus test (page 29) on the soil, and if needed, add powdered lime to make it more alkaline. The soil should be cool and moist, but not wet.

Crested Shield Fern, *Dryopteris cristata*

The crested shield fern has dark-green, leathery fronds from two to three feet tall and four to five inches wide. It is an attractive plant which looks charming tucked between rocks in a garden. Since the leaves are inclined to be brittle, the rocks are not only esthetic, but serve as a protective shield against strong winds.

Keep the soil moist at all times, but not wet, and use plenty of compost or peat to keep the soil slightly acid and light. The crested shield fern is found from Canada, south to Tennessee.

Intermediate Shield Fern, *Dryopteris intermedia*

The intermediate shield fern has graceful fronds two to three feet tall and eight to ten inches wide. It is not only a beautiful plant, but a sturdy one, and in some areas it is nearly everygreen.

It must be kept moist at all times and should be planted in soil mixed with plenty of compost to keep it loose and slightly acid. It is found from Canada throughout most of the northern United States, and south to Alabama.

Intermediate Shield Fern

Japanese Painted Fern, *Athyrium goeringianum*

Japanese painted fern, unlike most ferns, is softly multicolored, with muted hues that range from gray to a delicate rose, to many shades and gradations of green. This habit of variegation alone would make it an excellent selection for a shade garden, but it has other desirable qualities as well: a neat habit of growth, and leaves which are not only graceful but plentiful, and continue to unfurl throughout the summer. These leaves are about twenty inches tall and seven inches wide.

Lady Fern, *Athyrium filix-femina*

Lady fern is a wild fern which has become a popular cultivated garden plant. It is graceful, has a neat habit of growth, and is happy with soil that is neutral to slightly acid.

It grows to a height of two to three feet with fronds which are full and feathery. It is not a fast grower, and can be safely planted in a rock garden without fear of it "taking over." The soil should be kept moist, but not wet. Lady fern is found from Canada south to Virginia, and west to Colorado.

Common Maidenhair, *Adiantum pedatum*

The maidenhair is one of the daintiest of the hardy ferns and is a delight in both woodland and cultivated gardens. Its light green fronds grow in a fan shape on stems that reach ten to twelve inches high.

It grows best in acid soil enriched with compost or humus, and kept moist at all times. Maidenhair is found from Canada, south to Georgia, and west to Oklahoma.

Common Maidenhair

Spinulose Shield Fern, *Dryopteris spinulosa*

The spinulose shield fern, with fronds two feet long and six inches wide, is not only an attractive garden plant, but most useful for cutting. It is found in so many commercial flower arrangements that it is sometimes called "florist's fern."

Before autumn comes, you too can cut the fronds for future winter use by wrapping the cut stems with a damp paper towel, and placing the fronds in a plastic cleaner's bag before putting them in the refrigerator. The damp towel will provide enough moisture without permitting the fern to become wet. You can keep it fresh this way for an unusually long time.

Keep the soil of the spinulose shield fern constantly moist, but not wet, and plant in slightly acid, humus-rich soil. It is found from Canada, south to Virginia, and west to Missouri.

Ferns Which Must be Kept Wet

Interrupted Fern, *Osmunda claytoniana*

Unlike many ferns, the interrupted fern's name is an accurate description of the plant's fertile leaf. Its sterile fronds are full and graceful like its relative, the cinnamon fern. Its fertile fronds are

also full and graceful from the tip midway down the stem, but there the leaf pattern changes, and for a few inches there are leaves which are stunted and misshapen, thus giving the "interrupted" shape to the fertile leaf.

The plant grows about four feet tall and must be grown in acid soil in wet or swampy areas. It is a slow grower. It is found from eastern Canada south to Tennessee.

Marsh Fern, *Thelypteris palustris*

Marsh fern grows from one to three feet tall depending on the amount of light it receives. The farther it has to reach for light, the taller it grows. But its leaves don't widen as they lengthen, so the plant looks a little spindly if grown where it must compete for light.

To identify it in the woods, look for the difference between the sterile and fertile leaves. The sterile leaves appear strong, and are broad, full, and flat. The fertile leaves are thin and sparse and their edges seem to roll up, giving them a wilted look.

Marsh fern is a fast grower which spreads rapidly, and should be used in swampy or wet areas with slightly acid soil. It is found from Canada south to Tennessee, and west to Oklahoma.

Narrow-leaved Chain Fern, *Woodwardia areolata*

The narrow-leaved chain fern grows from eighteen to twenty-four inches high, and is a shining dark-green. It does not appear particularly graceful, but if you have a large area and need a fast-growing fern for wet or swampy conditions it is an ideal choice. Its underground rhizomes spread out rapidly, quickly forming a mat of lush greenery. The fern requires acid soil, and is found in swamplands from Canada to Florida, and west to Arkansas.

Royal Fern, *Osmunda regalis spectabilis*

Royal fern has a more feathery look than most ferns, and its leaves are four feet tall. It must grow in acid soil and be kept very wet. It spreads slowly and looks beautiful along the edge of a stream. Once established, it is a strong grower.

I grew mine along the edge of a river in Connecticut which

regularly went on a rampage, overflowing its banks and destroying everything in its path. But each time the flood receded, my lovely, light-green royal fern would bounce back. It even grew on rocks half-submerged in water where the only soil it had was what had clung to the root-mass as the water receded. Often I would find roots tucked under heavy boulders at the river's edge, making transplanting almost impossible.

Don't try to grow royal fern in your cultivated garden unless you can keep it sufficiently wet. The plant is found north from Canada, south to Florida, and west to Texas.

Virginia Chain Fern, *Woodwardia virginica*

Virginia chain fern is a rich green, and grows from three to four feet tall. It is an ideal selection for an acid, wet, or swampy area where a graceful, lush, fast-growing and rapidly spreading fern is desired. In fact, its underground rhizomes are so strong and dense that lifting them from the woods can be a difficult task. It strongly resembles the cinnamon fern. It is found from southeastern Canada south to Florida, and west to Texas.

Ferns Which Require Lime

Ebony Spleenwort (see page 59)
Bulblet Bladder Fern (see page 63)

4.

o-o-o-o-o-o-o-o-o-o

Flowers That Bloom in the Shade–Annuals as well as Perennials

The greatest challenge to success in a shady garden is to grow flowering plants, both annuals and perennials. To do this one must learn only one lesson: don't try to fool Mother Nature by thinking you can get roses, zinnias, marigolds, and other sun-loving plants to bloom in the shade. They won't.

Seed catalogs usually indicate which flowers bloom in sun, part sun, shade, half-shade, etc., but it's *you* who must create the proper light conditions needed to make your plants flower. The list of annuals and perennials included in this book were very carefully selected to flourish in almost any shade conditions, and should bloom if they get *two or three hours of sunshine each day along with strong light*. The more sun they get, of course, the more they will bloom.

If the shade is caused by tree branches, simply prune back those limbs that prevent sun and light from coming in. For this you need a good tree man, not a lumberjack. Trees do not have to be drastically cut to provide good light. Think of it as a thinning operation, not drastic surgery. Dappled sunlight will, in most cases, suffice. If you call your tree man when your trees are in full leaf, the job will be a lot easier. Have him climb high into the tree and judiciously trim as many branches as reasonably possible. He'll know to cut the dead limbs and branches that cross each other and double the density of the shade, but for the kind of sunlight you want, you must point the way. When you finally see the sun filtering through, you'll also see a better-looking, and eventually healthier tree. Be sure also to cut limbs that are closest to the ground. That will allow both the morning and late afternoon sun to come through. Let the light through all your trees; both they and the flowering plants will return the great favor.

Next on your agenda is the care and feeding of your soil. That's an absolute must under trees. The competition from a tree for water is considerable and becomes your second most difficult task in a tree-shaded garden. Work the soil under your trees as deeply as you can, preferably to a depth of two feet. Then mix the soil thoroughly with compost, leaf mold, or peat to hold moisture around your flowers, and add well-rotted manure (or the sterilized bag variety) to enrich the soil. If the soil is clay or heavy, add sand for good drainage.

The kind of trees your flowers are planted under should be thoroughly considered as well. If you have oak trees the soil will be acid, and you must select acid-loving plants such as primroses or cardinal flower, or continually add limestone or other alkaline-inducing chemicals. Under elms, ash, or locust trees the soil may be alkaline, and to bring it to a pH 6 or pH 7 (neutral), fertilizers such as ammonium sulphate, ammonium phosphate, and urea will give the soil a definite acid reaction. Most flowering annuals and perennials need a nearly neutral soil.

If your flower garden has a wall for a backdrop, just remember that the soil may be alkaline because the calcium in the wall is washed down by main rains. A wall may also give more shade than you want, but it is more an asset than a liability. It gives protection from strong winds and can provide a handsome background for your plants.

When I first started gardening, I despaired of the gardening books I read. Without exception, they all took it for granted that I knew about gardening and knew all the terminology. I did not. When the instructions called for mulching, I had to look up the meaning of the word. Then I had to find out which kind of mulch was the right one to use for my particular purpose. It took me more time to interpret the books than it did to follow through on their instructions. "Perennial" was a word I had to look up. Even though I was a city girl I did know that one meaning of the word "perennial" was "yearly," and for a while I really thought that perennials were another word for annuals. After all, "annual" means yearly, too. I learned the hard way. A glance at the dictionary is really confusing. Not only is "perennial" listed as "lasting the whole year through," but it is also defined as "lasting for an indefinitely long time," and "having a life cycle lasting more than two years." A gardener's definition is "a plant which lasts more than two years."

The gardener's definition of an annual is one that completes its life cycle within the space of one year. But what a year! Annuals are the most useful of all garden flowers because they bloom profusely all summer long in a wide variety of colors, forms, foliage, and fragrance. They can be used as edging plants, border plants, and background plants. They can be grown in hanging baskets, pots of all sizes, tubs, window boxes, planters, tree stumps, or anywhere color is needed and wanted all summer long. Annuals come to us from all parts of the world, are very cosmopolitan, and are therefore most adaptable. Most can adapt to winter greenhouses, too. And, they are easy to grow.

The most important rule to remember about any annual is the fact that it has but one blooming season. If you wish to prolong its bloom, it must be picked before it fades, or almost immediately after, so that no seed may form. A true annual has little root system and cannot store food for future use. It lives only to bloom quickly, set seed, and finish its existence (little realizing the joy it gives in its short life). Constant picking of its flowers gives it the energy to continue producing new blossoms to replace the ones removed.

The list of annuals I suggest in this book will grow in your shade garden if you follow the few rules I have outlined. However, the real trick in having lots of color in a heavily shaded garden is to grow pots and tubs of annuals and move them around—from filtered or full sun (if you have a spot and a strong back)—and then back into the shade again.

Many of the plants thought of as low-light indoor houseplants can be used as flowering annuals, annual shrubs, or vines. It's just a matter of changing your thinking. You purchase geraniums every year for bedding plants. Why not think of houseplants as summer bedding plants? For example, how about the wildly colored flowers of all the Gesnerias, including the Sinningias and Gloxinias, or

or the deliciously scented, white stephanotis. Plants with unusual foliage would be magnificent planted in a heavily shaded
garden. Consider asparagus fern, Pothos, or philodendron, trailing
from a planter with spathiphyllum, its white, lily-like flowers standing straight and tall. Or nephthytis cascading from a large tub with
a chamaedorea palm growing in the middle.

Some of the indoor ferns can be used as bedding plants too.
The holly fern (*Cyrtomium*) is neat and bushy, the bird's-nest fern
(*Asplenium*) makes a stately accent plant, and all the maidenhair
ferns (*Adiantum*) are graceful and airy.

The only disadvantage is that in many parts of the United
States—my area in New York for example—these plants can not be
set out until all danger of cold weather is past, and for me that
means June 15. But this problem is far outweighed by the advantages. All these plants can not only be brought into the house during winter to brighten it, but they will be healthier for having spent
the summer out-of-doors. And I haven't selected a single one
amongst them that will demand your sunny indoor window! That's
a real bonus!

A perennial plant is "herbaceous," which means its foliage disappears at the end of its growing season, and the plant lives underground in winter waiting for spring to renew its growth. Perennial's
long life, their dependable habits, and their yearly display of beauty
make them the most reliable of all garden flowers. Sometimes it is
hard to believe that all of them were wildflowers at one time. Careful cultivation and hybridization through the years have changed
many of them so much that it is often difficult to trace their ancestry.
The results of those years of careful cultivation have made the
plants more vigorous, the flowers larger and often more varied, and
above all, more breathtakingly beautiful than ever before.

Because today's perennials are so nearly perfect, your use of
them must be carefully planned in order to display that perfection
in your garden. No planting plan requires more thought, more
study, or more skill. Here is where your own creative talent and
knowledge can come to the fore. The list of perennials, and their
description, color, size, and time of bloom, must be studied carefully because you'll want a succession of bloom all summer long.
You'll really have to chart your garden on paper first. And this is
really the hardest part of a perennial garden. Even weeding is easier!

Make it easy for yourself by planting together those flowers which require similar care or soil. Don't plant only one or two of each kind either. Big, bold masses give the greatest effect. If you want to keep your initial cost down (and who doesn't), don't plant too closely together. Most perennials can be divided every other year, and if you can afford to be patient, you'll get additional plants at no extra cost. Don't make your perennial bed too narrow or it will look skimpy. On the other hand, don't make it too wide either or you won't be able to get in to it for weeding. Six feet is an easy width to handle. Spare no effort in preparing your soil thoroughly with a well-balanced fertilizer and humus. Remember, a perennial garden is forever.

Another term, often found in garden catalogs, that can be confusing is "biennial." A biennial is a plant that requires two years to bloom from seed, and dies in the second year, after blooming.

FLOWERING PERENNIALS

Astilbe, *Astilbe*

Astilbes, which are sometimes called spirea, are a real joy in a shade garden, and in my opinion, they are one of the loveliest of any of the perennials. They are graceful, colorful, and sturdy. There are over forty-five hybrid varieties which range in size from six inches to three feet. The flowers resemble light, feathery plumes and come in a myriad of colors—red, rose, pink, salmon, lilac, white, and cream. The bloom stays on the plant through autumn, gradually taking on a darker hue.

The trick to keeping them beautiful is to be sure that the soil stays moist. Before you plant, work the soil thoroughly and mix a lot of peat, compost, leaf mold, or some sort of humus into it so that it will retain moisture. Use some sand too, for good drainage. Each year work a little more compost into the soil around the plants. Do it gently though, as their roots are near the surface. To propagate the plant, divide it in the spring.

Some good hybrids:

A. 'Avalanche' has pure white flowers on eighteen inch stems.
A. 'Deutschland' has extra large, white flowers on twenty-four inch stems.

A. 'Europa' has pink flowers and grows about eighteen to twenty-four inches tall.

A. 'Fanal' has brilliant carmine-red flowers and grows about eighteen inches high.

A. 'Ostrich Plume' has salmon-pink plumes and reaches a forty-inch height.

A. 'Red Sentinel' has rich red flowers and grows twenty-four to thirty inches high.

Bergenia, *Bergenia cordifolia*

Named after Karl August von Berger, the eighteenth-century botanist, bergenia is a showy plant and makes a striking accent in a perennial shade garden because it has handsome foliage which resembles the leaves of a water lily. In the spring it has pink or white flowers which grow in heavy clusters almost like a nosegay. The plant grows in a clump not more than a foot high, but because of the size of the leaves with their thick, fleshy look, it appears to be a much larger plant.

Plant it in very rich moist soil and do not let it dry out. In the winter, cover it with a protective layer such as leaves.

Bergenia

Bleeding Heart, *Dicentra* (see also Chapter 3, page 32)

There are several species of bleeding heart. All are graceful, with slender arching stems festooned with heart-shaped flowers and delicate fern-like foliage. All should grow in cool moist soil thoroughly mixed with leaf mold or compost.

D. eximia is the shortest, growing only to about twelve inches, and has rosy-purple blooms in May and again in September. There is a white variety called *alba*.

D. spectabilis is the charming, old-fashioned bleeding heart with rosy-red, heart-shaped flowers which grow from 1½ to 2 feet tall. It blooms only in the spring and, unfortunately, disappears in the late summer.

D. formosa is similar to *D. eximia* but has coarser foliage and pink flowers.

Candytuft, *Iberis sempervirens*

Candytuft is a tidy, low-growing plant with dense, dark evergreen foliage. In the spring it has charming little white flowers which completely cover the plant. It is a marvelous plant to use for edging, and has varieties which range in size from six inches to

twelve inches. It has no special soil requirements, but does best in a rich garden soil.

Candytuft will bloom indoors in winter. Carefully dig strong plants in the early autumn, and plant them in a pot with a mixture of soil, peat, and perlite. Sink the pot into the ground and leave for four to six weeks in cold weather. Bring it into the house and leave it in the coldest room you have—like an unheated porch. Gradually move it into warmer rooms, and to a sunny window. As the Latin name *sempervirens* indicates, the plant is always green.

Cardinal Flower, *Lobelia cardinalis, Lobelia siphilitica*

Lobelia is a very showy plant with striking scarlet or blue flowers which grow on spikes from one to two feet tall. They are much prized in either woodland or cultivated gardens, and require careful attention to their soil and watering. Incorporate plenty of leaf mold or peat into a rich soil when you plant one, and never allow the plant to dry out. They naturalize well near the edge of a woodland pond. Lobelias were named after Matthias de Lobel, physician to King James I.

L. siphilitica (blue lobelia) has lovely blue flowers and is the easiest of the two to grow in the shade. It blooms in August and September.

L. cardinalis is more spectacular, with brilliant scarlet-colored
flower spikes. It blooms in July and August.

Chinese Bellflower or Balloonflower, *Platycodon grandiflorum*

Bellflower and balloonflower are not only the common names
of this delightful perennial, but are also very descriptive of the
flower. Branching, two-foot stems carry many blooms which swell
like balloons in the bud stage and later split open to become a five-
petaled, bell-shaped flower. The flowers, which bloom from June
to September, are usually a deep blue, but there is a white variety
called *albus*.

It is a good border plant provided it has well-drained soil.
Staking is necessary unless you use a dwarf variety like *mariesii*
which grows only about one foot tall. The plant gets its botanical
name from the Greek *platys* meaning "broad," and *kodon* meaning
"bell."

Chinese Bellflower

Christmas Rose, *Helleborus niger*

Despite its name, don't expect to find the Christmas rose blooming before the middle or end of January. But, in the east where no other flowers appear in winter, it is one of nature's won-

ders to find the lovely Christmas rose with its fresh, white, saucer-shaped flowers pushing up from the crown of the plant through the snow, surrounded by its deep-green, almost evergreen foliage.

The Christmas rose doesn't like to be moved, so prepare the soil carefully before planting. Make a wide, two-foot-deep hole and add a mixture of equal parts of rich soil, well-rotted manure (the sterilized bag type will do), peat moss, and sand. Propagate by division. If you start your plants from seed, be prepared to be patient; they probably won't bloom for two to three years.

The blossoms can be used for floral arrangements, but take a candle with you to the garden and burn the open end of the stem as soon as it is cut. Although the flower is attractive in a vase, I dislike to cut mine because, left in the garden, they sometimes stay until March or April.

Helleborus orientalis, called lenten rose, is dark-purple, blooms around Lent, and is not nearly as nice a plant as Christmas rose.

Columbine, *Aquilegia caerulea, Aquilegia canadensis*

I remember columbines in my grandmother's garden. It is a charming old-fashioned 2½ foot plant and has delicate lavender-blue or vanilla-white flowers with long, slender spurs. Columbines are good for cutting. Since grandmother's day there have been many new hybrids which are more vigorous and last longer. Give all of them a good garden soil and do not allow it to dry out. They will propagate themselves if you let the seed self-sow around the parent plant. You can also divide the plant in the fall.

A. caerulea has lavender flowers, and is the state flower of Colorado.

A. caerulea 'Mrs. Nicols' has blue, long-spurred flowers and grows thirty inches tall.

A. canadensis has lemon-yellow flowers and is sometimes called the American or Canadian columbine.

Some new hybrids:

A. chrysantha has golden-yellow flowers and is a nice, bushy plant.

A. chrysantha 'Silver Queen' has pure-white flowers which bloom for a long season.

A. 'Crimson Star' has long crimson spurs with white centers, tinged with red.

A. 'Rose Queen' has flowers in shades of rose.

Day Lily, *Hemerocallis*

I once visited a beautiful home garden which was ablaze with blooms and color, and yet there were no flowering plants other than day lilies. The owners had chosen the varieties carefully, planted them thoughtfully, and had blossoms from spring through summer and right into fall. There are thousands of varieties available today in almost every color—pink, red, green, white, yellow—which bloom at different times of the year. They are a far cry from the common orange variety which grows wild by the roadside.

Day lilies are an asset to any garden. They grow about three feet tall in graceful clumps with elegant, slender arching foliage. Each strong flowering stalk has many buds which open for one day only—hence the name, but there is such a profusion of buds opening in succession that the plant seems to be in constant bloom. They are good for cutting and the buds continue to open one at a time,

even after they are cut. Left in the same position, day lilies get larger and more beautiful, but every few years they should be divided to strengthen the plant, and to encourage propagation. They are not too fussy about soil and do well in any good garden loam, but soil enriched with manure and peat is ideal.

For more information about day lilies write:

The American Hemerocallis Society
Signal Mountain, Tennessee 37377
Dues: $7.50 per annum

Fairy Bell, *Disporum*

The Fairy bell plant is not well-known or seen too often. It looks a little like false Solomon's seal (page 37), with bunches of yellow-green tubular or bell-shaped flowers hanging from the axils of arching stems. It blooms in May and, depending on the variety, grows from 1 to 2½ feet tall.

The plant requires a good garden soil which must be kept moist. It can be propagated in March by division.

Fairy Bell

Foxglove, *Digitalis*

Foxglove is a proud-looking plant, standing straight and tall at 2½ feet with long spikes of purple, pink, or white flowers. It gets its botanical name from the Latin *digitus* or "finger," because the individual flowers on the spike look like a gloved finger. The flowers generally grow on one side of the spike only, but the newer Excelsior strain has flowers all around the stem, and they come in a wider variety of colors; orchid, rose, apricot, cream, and white.

Because its seed sows itself and returns the following year, I have included it with perennials, but it is actually a biennial (a plant which requires two years to complete its life cycle). There is a perennial form, *D. grandiflora,* with large, pale-yellow flowers, but it is better to regard this variety as a biennial.

Foxglove is a good plant for drying. Use a commercial mix such as Flower Dri, Dryonex, or even kitty litter. You can also make your own by mixing two parts cornmeal to one part borax. However, Flower Dri is the fastest. The flower spike should be buried in the mix for two to three weeks (depending on the drying mixture you use), and when removed, a wire stem can be taped on for extra length.

Foxgloves require good garden soil and plenty of moisture. Sow the seeds in midsummer for blooming in the following spring. Plants can be divided in spring.

Fuchsia, *Fuchsia magellanica*

One of the loveliest plants for a hanging basket or window box is the exquisite fuchsia with its dainty little flowers which resemble a chorus line of ballet dancers. It grows a few feet tall, and in the summer it is festooned with pendant ruby-red, blue, or purple blooms until stopped by frost. There is a hardy variety that will grow outdoors as far north as New York City or Connecticut, if given a protected location.

Carl Totemeir, Director of the famous gardens at Old West-

Fuchsia makes an effective, unusual hedge.

bury, wrote to me about his experience of growing *Fuchsia magellanica* in the shade. He said,

> *Fuchsia magellanica* has done well in the garden in half or filtered shade and in full sun as well. Where it has been planted in heavy shade however, it has become very straggly and sparsely flowered. The best foliage color and appearance is when it is planted in partial shade. In full sunlight the foliage becomes somewhat yellow.

Fuchsia magellanica likes rich, loamy, well-drained soil. Don't forget to plant it in a protected position, and in the winter protect it with a layer of dry leaves.

Gentiana, *Gentiana acaulis* and *Geniana andrewsii*

There are several species of gentians, and *G. acaulis* and *G. andrewsii* are the most popular and easiest to grow. They are woodland flowers which can be brought into the perennial border. The flower spikes of both species have dark-blue or purple (remember gentian-violet in your paint set) tubular flowers, but *G. acaulis* grows only four inches tall while *G. andrewsii* is 1½ feet tall.

The plant is named after Gentius, King of Illyria, who is credited with the discovery of the medicinal value of the roots. The species from which the bitter tonic is made is *G. lutea*.

Gentians prefer a cool, moist, or marshy soil, and look beautiful when planted at the edge of a shaded bog pond. They are easy to grow from seeds.

Gentian

Leopard's-bane, *Doronicum plantagineum*

Leopard's-bane looks like a yellow daisy with heart-shaped leaves. To be effective in a cultivated garden, plants should be grown in a gigantic mass. They bring color to your perennial border early in the spring. Unfortunately, the leaves die back in the summer after they bloom, so plant something evergreen nearby. It is a fine plant to cut flowers from, and if you snip regularly you are apt to get a second growth of flowers in the autumn.

Grow these two-foot plants in good garden soil lightened with peat or some sort of humus. Divide every few years when the plant has finished flowering.

Leopard's-bane got its name from an old legend. The juice of the root was supposed to be poisonous and used to tip arrows when hunting leopards. (I can't vouch for the accuracy of this since I've never shot a leopard.)

There are two good varieties with large three-inch flowers; 'Harpur Crewe,' and 'Miss Mason.'

Monkshood or Autumn Aconite, *Aconitum fischeri, Aconitum wilsonii*

Monkshood is a showy two-to-four-foot erect plant with many little purple-blue, helmet-shaped flowers growing on a sturdy stalk. Its dark-green foliage is coarsely toothed and most effective in the garden. It's great for providing a little color late in the season since it blooms from August to October. *A. wilsonii* has deeper violet flowers than *A. fischeri.*

The plant must be kept moist in rich, cool soil to which plenty of compost or leaf mold has been added. It is inclined to get mildew in the summer, but that can be controlled with flowers of sulphur, which can be bought at a gardener's store.

Seed may be sown in April, or the plant can be divided in spring or autumn. However, be careful about this because once the plant has been established in your garden it doesn't like moving about, and may take a year or two before it will bloom again. If it is very cold in your area cover the plant with leaves in the winter.

Although you are not likely to, don't eat the root which looks much like horse-radish; it's poisonous.

New York Aster, *Aster novi-belgi*

The New York aster most commonly seen is a tall blue plant with a daisy-type flower which grows about three feet tall. But since the days of the late Ernest Ballard who did so much to hybridize this plant, there are over seventy-five varieties. They grow from six inches to five feet and are white, pink, mauve, crimson, or purple in both single and double forms.

Asters are not fussy about the soil they grow in, but in the shade the soil should be lightened with peat moss. They bloom late in September or October. The taller varieties will require staking, particularly 'Eventide,' which has violet flowers so large they weigh down the branches. They grow quite quickly and may need dividing every two or three years.

Primrose, *Primula*

"Come my love, we'll walk the primrose path . . . " One of the dividends of having a shade garden is the ability to grow the charming primrose of poet's fame.

The *Primula* is a large plant genus with species and varieties from six inches to two feet tall. All have clusters of bell-like flowers, some of which grow in candelabra fashion on tall stems, others in whorls on stout stems. Some bloom in early spring, others right into summer. Some are fragrant, others are not. The plant gets its name from the Latin word *primus* meaning "first," referring to their early spring flowering habit.

Primroses come in a wide selection of colors—vivid shades of red, intense purple, and orange, or cool tints of white, blue, or lilac. In addition to shade there is one requirement common to all —they must grow in moist soil. Some species require more moisture than others, but it is only a matter of degree.

When planting, dig a hole twice as large as your roots require since they need plenty of room for spreading out, and mix a trowelfull of manure with the soil in the bottom of the hole. Use a great deal of mulch to retain moisture, but do not cover the crown of the plant. Do not pack the plants down with leaves for protection in the winter. They do not like smothering. If they grew in a place exposed to strong winter wind and sun, put discarded Christmas tree branches over them. More damage is done by overprotecting than underprotecting since they are hardy alpine plants.

P. alpicola is one of my favorite species because it blooms so much later than the others—in June and July—and because it has a delightful fragrance. It has nice, tall twelve-to-fourteen-inch stems, and flowers of white, yellow, or rose.

P. auricula is the primrose usually seen at the florist's with the bell-shaped fragrant flowers. All of the hybrids from this variety are handsome. Outdoors they do particularly well in a rock garden where they receive a natural amount of winter protection. In the summer, the rocks help keep their roots cool. Flowers have a white or yellow eye with petals of yellow or red. They bloom in April and May and grow about nine inches tall.

P. denticulata is one of the easiest primroses to grow and does well

when started from seed. It grows twelve inches tall and has
lilac or mauve flowers. Be sure it has good drainage or it will
get crown rot. It blooms from March to May.

P. japonica is a beautiful candelabra species which grows two feet
tall. You may be disappointed if you try to use it as a border
plant in your cultivated garden since it requires an exceptional
amount of moisture. It is easier grown in a woodland garden,
and there it will self-seed. The flowers are purple and white.
It blooms from May to July.

P. polyantha is the most popular primrose of all, and for good reason. It is extremely hardy, grows in almost any soil, has large
clusters of lovely flowers on ten inch stems, and comes in a
myriad of tints and tones. It blooms in May and is spectacular.

P. rosea is a particularly charming early bloomer only six inches
tall, with clusters of brilliant rose flowers. It should be kept
exceptionally moist. If you wish to transplant or divide, do so
in early spring. It blooms from April through May.

P. vulgaris is the species seen most often growing naturally in the
woods, and comes in a wide variety of colors—pink, red, and
cream. Some are double. The plant is six inches tall, and blooms
from March through April.

For more information about primroses write to:

> The American Primrose Society
> 7100 S.W. 209th
> Beaverton, Oregon 97005
> Dues: $5.00 per annum

Shooting Star, *Dodecatheon meadia*

Shooting star grows wild in many parts of the country, and is
a colorful addition in the cultivated perennial garden. It is a spring
flower which grows ten to fifteen inches tall and has about twenty
cyclamen-like white or pink flowers which grow on each erect stem.
The leaves are a six-inch oval and grow close to the ground.

Shooting star should be grown in acid, well-drained, wood-
land-type soil that is rich in humus and leaf mold, and it should be
kept thoroughly moist throughout the summer. Plants are propagated best by division.

There are two native Californian species: *D. hendersonii* which has fewer dark-purple flowers, and *D. jeffryei,* a larger plant with red flowers.

Windflower, *Anemone japonica, Anemone vitifolia*

Anemones are graceful plants with delicate-looking, strongly colored flowers which are excellent for cutting. There are many species, but the two included here are particularly useful since they bloom at different times and maintain color for a longer period in your garden. Anemones get their name from the Greek word *anemos* or "wind," because the flowers move so gracefully in the wind.

A. japonica has pink, red, purple, or white flowers, and grows about 1½ to 2 feet tall. It blooms in September or October. Two charming varieties are 'Queen Charlotte,' a beautiful pink; and 'whirlwind,' a lovely semi-double white.

A vitifolia has white flowers with large, heart-shaped leaves and blooms in July.

Both species should be given as much light as possible in your shade garden, and should be grown in good soil lightened with peat or leaf mold. Propagate by root cuttings.

ANNUALS

Beard Tongue, *Pentstemon*

Pentstemon is a 2½-foot tall plant which is an annual in my New York area, but a perennial in warmer climates. It resembles a foxglove in shape, with showy, bugle-shaped flowers of red, rose, pink, lavender, or white. It requires a little more sun than many of the other annuals listed here, but I included it because it is so very tolerant of dry soil—an unusual advantage.

It gets its botanical name from the Greek *pente* (five) and *stemon* (stamen), because the flowers have five stamens.

P. hartwegii is particularly lovely, and has scarlet or blood-red drooping flowers.

P. 'Firebird' has brilliant crimson flowers.
P. 'Alice Hindley' is a pale-blue rose.
P. 'White Bedder' is white.

Browallia, *Browallia speciosa major*

Browallia is a charming blue, purple, or white annual which blooms profusely on shapely stems. The plant forms round compact mounds with glossy, emerald-green foliage. It is easy to grow,

and because it doesn't get more than eight to ten inches tall, is excellent for borders, beds, window boxes, or pots. It likes moist, porous soil. After blooming all summer in the garden, browallia can be potted and brought indoors to bloom all winter.

B. 'Velvet Bells' has deep-blue, plush-like flowers.
B. 'Silver Bells' is a pure, glistening snow-white.
B. 'Powder Blue' is a true-blue.

Butterfly Flower, *Schizanthus pinnatus*

Butterfly flower is sometimes called the poor man's orchid because each flower looks like a tiny orchid. Although it is often used as an indoor potted plant for winter bloom, outdoors it is a lovely, summer-blooming, annual bedding plant. It grows from one to two feet tall, branches freely, and is almost smothered with delicate orchid-like blooms in salmon, light-pink, carmine, scarlet, lilac, or violet, with exotic contrasting (throat) markings.

S. 'Angel Wings' has lovely butterfly-like blossoms which cover the uniform compact, conical, one-foot plants. Blooms may be pink or lavender with a distinct yellow center.
S. 'Hit Parade' has masses of large delicate blooms which almost completely cover the plant, in a wide range of colors from white to gold. It looks great in a window box.

Coleus

Coleus is a plant famous for its wildly colored leaves splashed with red, green, white, pink, yellow, and burgundy, in all kinds of bright or subtle combinations and patterns. Some have huge, exotic leaves in rich, luxurious color arrangements; others have abundant, narrow, deeply serrated leaves, or billowing lacy leaves painted with red, purple, and green. There is a new hybrid called "Carefree" which has brightly colored leaves lobed like an oak leaf. There is even a black coleus.

Don't grow this plant for its flowers. In fact, pinch them off as soon as you see them if you want to keep the plant beautiful, full, and bushy. The beauty of this plant is in its flashy leaves. Before the cold weather begins, pot some for indoor winter color.

C. 'Pink Brilliant' blends coral-pink and coppery-salmon and has a narrow green border.

C. 'Red Brilliant' has a red maple-leaf center surrounded by maroon, and edged in light-green.

C. 'Sunset Glory' is a glowing orange with a narrow, green edge.

C. salicifolius is a small, mound-shaped plant eight to ten inches high with narrow, deeply serrated leaves. It comes in shades of yellow or red.

C. 'Magic Lace' has billowing leaves of royal-red and purple,

splashed with bright greens and yellows. The leaf edges are deeply serrated with lace-like notches.

C. 'Othello' is a black coleus with satiny-black, crinkled leaves.

C. 'Gold Dust' has extra large exotic leaves flecked with yellow.

C. 'Red Monarch' has luxurious, oversized vermillion leaves.

C. 'Carefree Jade' has an ivory center blending to a green edge.

C. 'Carefree Pink' has a phlox-pink center with a narrow, green edge.

Impatiens, *Impatiens balsamina, Impatiens sultanii,* and the New Guinea Impatiens

A mass planting of impatiens in a shade garden is a glorious sight. This little plant is not only one of the most dependable of all flowering annuals in shade gardens, it also has so many blooms at one time that an area of it is a riot of color. Planted carefully with one shade blending into another, a garden of impatiens can easily resemble an artist's palette of colors—white, orange, salmon, scarlet, purple, pink, rose, red, and tangerine. Some are even two-tone, candy-striped red or pink. There are dwarf varieties growing in bushy mounds no more than six inches high. There are new double impatiens with flowers that look like little roses in shades of white, plum, appleblossom pink, rose, or vermillion.

It is no wonder that out of a total annual retail value of 150 million dollars for ornamental bedding plants, impatiens accounts for 3 million dollars or 2 percent. And, according to the National Bedding Plant Producers Association, the percentage of impatiens in relation to other kinds of plants is increasing each year. In the eastern United States, according to the United States Department of Agriculture, it is the most popular bedding plant for shady and semishaded moist areas. Of the more than twenty-five botanical gardens, arboretums, public gardens, and horticultural societies who cooperated with me in the regional section of this book (p. 196), over half of them chose impatiens as an annual for "full shade."

They are easily grown from seed, and begin to bloom three months from sowing. There is seed tape available too. This water-soluble tape, which has the seed properly spaced and imbedded in it, dissolves instantly with the first watering, leaving the seeds in firm contact with the growing medium. The tape can be cut into small lengths to fit any size box, pot, or container. If your local store doesn't have it, write to G.W. Park Seed Company in Greenwood, South Carolina 29647.

There are also pelleted seeds. When the seeds are very small, some nurseries coat them with a shell to make them larger and easier to handle. You can place the seed pellets exactly where you want them, and even minute seeds become easy to handle. The coating dissolves in the moist soil.

The seed catalogs devote page after page to Impatiens. Some interesting varieties are described below.

I. *'Shady Lady'* is a mound-shaped twelve-to-fifteen-inch plant with 1¾-to-2-inch flowers in great profusion. It is available in white, orange, salmon, scarlet, red, and rose.

I. *'Crazy Quilt'* has flowers in contrasting bicolors of white interspersed with each plant's basic flower color—cherry-red, scarlet, rose, orange, and pink.

I. *'Tangeglow'* has large, two-inch, tangerine-colored flowers on eighteen inch plants.

I. *'Huckabuc'* is a dwarf, spreading plant ten inches wide with white and orchid bicolored flowers.

I. *'Royal Rose'* has double flowers of crimson on one-foot plants.

I. *'Azalea Queen'* has double flowers with luscious apricot darts in the center. The plants grow one foot high.

I. 'Scarlet Baby' is a dwarf, compact plant which grows only six inches tall and has brilliant red flowers.

I. 'Pink Baby' has bright-pink flowers on tiny six-inch plants.

Now, if all this variety were not enough, there are major new developments in the impatiens world. Since the turn of the century, botanists have known there were extraordinary impatiens in New Guinea because a few of the plants were grown in some conservatories. But the seeds were almost impossible to collect in New Guinea because the mature seed capsules would explode at the slightest touch, scattering the seeds in all directions. Cuttings did not survive the trip across the ocean. Luckily, in 1970, two plant explorers from the United States Department of Agriculture, Harold Winters and Joseph Higgins, went to New Guinea on a grant from the Longwood Foundation, and personally brought back many cuttings. Twenty-five survived. By February 1972 the Department of Agriculture was ready to release what they called the "New Guinea Impatiens Collection" to selected nurserymen, plant breeders, and other scientists. A few were offered for sale by nurserymen in 1973 and 1974.

The New Guinea collection offers a wealth of new genetic characteristics not seen in impatiens now grown in the United States. For one thing the stems are much stouter and sturdier, and the leaves have greater coloration—some with variegated foliage and others with croton-like foliage. The flowers, although not as profuse, are much larger (up to 2½ inches wide) than those we have on plants grown commercially today. Plants from the New Guinea collection were given to me for experimentation, and they have not proved to be as tolerant of shade as the ordinary impatiens. The collection is presently being evaluated by seedsmen for possible development of seed-propagated varieties.

Some of the Longwood hybrid Impatiens are listed below.

I. 'Carousel' has leaves with yellow centers, green edges, and red mid-veins. Its flowers are orange-red, 2⅛ inches in diameter.

I. 'Painted Lady' has dark-green leaves and two-inch, pinkish-white flowers.

I. 'Lolipop' has 2½-inch, bright, orange-pink blossoms which offer a superb floral display.

I. 'Big Top' is the best of all the white impatiens to be developed at Longwood Gardens, and the plant, when in full bloom, literally covers itself with large, flat, round, white 2½-inch flowers.

The New Guinea collection being developed by the United States Department of Agriculture is a little different.

I. linearifolia has variegated green, yellow, and red, long, narrow leaves, and salmon-pink flowers 1¼ inches in diameter.

I. herzogii K. Schum has bronze-green foliage with white-eyed, orange flowers which are 1½ inches in diameter.

*I. 'Mt. Hagen '*has glossy leaves with an area of yellow at the base. It is not a spectacular bloomer, but doesn't need flowers to be attractive because the leaves are so colorful.

I. 'Korn Farm' has dark, metallic, reddish-green leaves and is 2½ inches in diameter. It is named for the Korn Farm Tree Nursery.

Monkey Flower, *Mimulus*

Monkey flower is a perky, summer-blooming annual which doesn't grow more than six to twelve inches tall, and makes an attractive window box, edging, or bedding plant. It can also be used indoors for winter bloom.

M. brevipes has yellow flowers.
M. 'Red Emperor' has large red flowers.
M. fremonrii has crimson flowers.

M. 'Queens' has extra-large flowers which are richly spotted.

The Monarch strain grows twelve inches tall, has giant flowers, and comes in a wonderful range of colors.

Salvia or Scarlet Sage, *Salvia*

Salvia is a brilliant bedding or edging plant which blooms from early summer until the winter frost, but puts on its best show late in the summer. Most varieties need to be grown in full sun to bring out their fiery colors. However, the pastel-colored salvias, which come in some of the nicest jewel-toned colors, actually do better in the shade. So be careful when you choose your seeds or rooted cuttings, so that you get the variety needed for your shade garden. Salvias grow in little clumps from six to twenty inches tall, and have showy spikes covered with colored puffs of tubular flowers.

Those listed below are all suitable for a shade garden.

S. 'Lavender Love' has long, full-flowered spikes of rich lavender. It grows eighteen inches tall.

S. 'Snowkist' has clear red flowers with white stripes, and grows twenty inches tall.

S. 'White Fire' has creamy white flowers and grows fourteen inches tall.

S. 'Rose Flame' has rich, coral-rose flower spikes. It grows two feet tall.

S. 'Salmon Pygmy' has salmon-pink flowers and grows only six
inches tall.

Wax Begonia, *Begonia semperflorens*

Wax begonias are an everblooming border, bedding, or edging
plant with brightly colored, many-hued flowers covering neat,
mound-like plants whose foliage, in many cases, is as colorful as the
bloom. Formerly, the plants did better in full sun, but in recent
years there has been much hybridization and now wax begonias
come high on the list of shade-loving annuals. There are dwarf
and semi-dwarf forms; some with green leaves, and others bronze
or variegated. Some are covered with little blooms, others have
large, three-inch blooms. Still other flowers are double.

All varieties prefer a loose, moist soil, and for bushy plants in
the shade, all should be pinched back. Remove dead flowers to encourage heavy blooming. Before the first frost, pot some for indoor
winter bloom.

B. 'Red Wonder' has scarlet flowers.
B. 'Linda Bright' has pink flowers.
B. 'Rose Perfection' has deep-rose flowers.
B. 'Ball Red' has orange-scarlet flowers.
B. 'Melody' has salmon-pink flowers.

LARGE FLOWERED WAX BEGONIAS

B. *'Butterfly'* has red, white, pink, or deep-rose flowers.

VARIEGATED WAX BEGONIAS

B. *'Calla Queen'* has bright-scarlet flowers and variegated green and white leaves.

DOUBLE WAX BEGONIAS

B. *'Blushing Baby'* has light-pink flowers.
B. *'Christmas Candle'* has rose-red flowers.
B. *'White Christmas'* has ivory flowers.

Wishbone Flower, *Torenia*

Wishbone flower is very versatile. It is an excellent annual bedding, border, or edging plant, which blooms from June until the winter frost. It is equally delightful as a pot plant which blooms year round. It is an easily grown, prolific, bushy, one-foot plant. Its flowers, which are blue or white, resemble something between a pansy and a tiny iris.

T. *'Bicolor'* comes from Italy, and is a mixture of blue and white.
T. *fournieri nana compacta* is a dwarf variety not more than eight inches tall, and very useful as an edging plant. It can be either blue or white.

5

❁❁❁❁❁❁❁❁❁❁❁

Mother Nature's own Cosmetic– Ground Covering Plants

Like any good make-up, ground covering plants are Mother Nature's own cosmetic; they cover imperfections and they beautify. They are most useful in a shady garden because they are much more satisfactory and dependable than grass (less work), and their textures are far more interesting. Ground covering plants are easy to grow. They require little care or maintenance and they are less prone to disease than most plants. Even the United States Department of Highway uses them for roadway median dividers. In California, algerian ivy was the choice of the Highway Department. In a previous book, *The Ivy Book*, I described sixty different varieties of ivy.

Ground covering plants keep the areas they are in looking very neat and tidy. They keep fallen leaves from blowing away, and by so doing add to the humus content of their soil. It usually takes a year or more for ground covers to become established, but once they do they are more or less permanent, and that means one less chore for you.

Many gardeners only think of ground covering plants for areas where grass will not grow—under shallow, rooted trees such as maple or beech. The creative gardener, however, will think of them as a charming transition—a change of texture and color between grass and shrubs. Ground covers can fill small areas not large enough for shrubs. Old tree stumps can be turned into a patch of brightness by allowing an interesting and unusual ivy such as 'Manda's Crested' to wind its graceful way over it. The right kind of ground cover, leucothoë for example, can soften the line of a path and make it look even more inviting. A combination of ground covers such as periwinkle and hosta can bring unexpected and cheerful bloom in partial shade from May until autumn. The soft lavender-blue periwinkle displays its color in May and June, and is followed by the lush leaves and tall flowers of the hosta until autumn. I can't believe anything can beat the combination of dainty ivy and lily of the valley as a ground cover in continual shade. Together they become a symphony of texture and form. Creeping thyme or Nepeta can be used between cracks in walks or between steppingstones to make your garden more attractive, and to control weeds. Pachistima or hosta can edge a flower border with grace and charm. And nothing looks better on a bank or slope than euonymus, and it also helps to prevent soil erosion.

Of course, pachysandra is by all odds the most popular ground cover and it certainly deserves its popularity. But the extra dividends, in the form of flowers or berries, from many other ground covering plants warrants a closer examination of them. A few pages ahead twenty-nine shade-loving ground covers are described in detail. There is something for every situation. Some are evergreen,

After several attempts to grow grass in this shady area, the author planted pachysandra, which has become a thick, lush ground cover.

which have the advantage of keeping your garden a lovely green all winter long which, of course, is ideal. But, if you live in an area where snow covers the ground most of the winter and it doesn't matter if your ground cover disappears, consider the list of herbaceous plants. There's a marvelous variety and some are most unusual. Although these lose their leaves in the winter, they come back in the spring sparkling, fresh, and lovely.

Ground covering plants are usually easy to propagate. If some plants should die, it's easy to move another in. The soil should be well-prepared before planting. This means a soil which has good moisture retention as well as drainage, and this can be done by incorporating peat and sand into your soil. Work soil at least six inches deep and add a complete fertilizer before planting. 5–10–5 is ideal. For every one thousand square feet add twenty to forty pounds. The numbers on the bag of plant food refer to the proportions of the three main soil elements used by plants. If it is 5–10–5 it means that five percent of the contents is nitrogen, ten percent is phosphorus, and five percent is potash. The elements are always listed in that order.

Since I'm a ground cover fancier from way back, I can tell you my favorites loud and clear.

EVERGREEN GROUND COVERS

Best all around—ivy
Best for banks—euonymous
Most unusual—leucothoë
Good flowers—vinca
Best for rock gardens—wintergreen
Best for cracks between stones—creeping thyme

HERBACEOUS GROUND COVERS

Best all around—sweet woodruff, hosta, or epimedium
Fastest growing—lamium
Most spectacular flowers—hosta or iris cristata
Best for rock gardens—lily of the valley
Best low creeper—Nepeta

EVERGREEN GROUND COVERS

Cowberry, *Vaccinium vitis-idaea*

There are several varieties of cowberry—low-bush blueberry, mountain cranberry, shore cranberry. All are evergreen if grown in poor acid soil; if not, they are deciduous. They thrive in the northern part of the United States and do not like hot, dry weather. They grow from eight inches to one foot, and have pink or white flowers that are followed by small red berries in the fall.

It is not a particularly pretty or elegant plant, but it is very useful for two reasons—it will cover the ground where little else will grow, and the birds love it. If your garden is a bird sanctuary, cowberry is a good choice.

Cowberry

Creeping Thyme, *Thymus serpyllum*

Creeping thyme is a tiny plant which grows no more than one inch high, and is ideal for use on a path between steppingstones because it hugs the ground. Used instead of grass, the path will keep its neat appearance and never have to be mowed.

Although it does well in the shade, it does better if it receives some sun and strong light, and it is such a useful creeper it is worth

cutting a few branches from a tree that might be shading it. Creeping thyme has small violet flowers, and its tiny leaves have a delightful aroma when crushed. It is hardy as far north as New York or Michigan.

Drooping Leucothoë, *Leucothoë catesbaei*

Drooping leucothoë is really a shrub, but I have found that with sharp pruning it becomes one of the most attractive ground covers I know. Left unpruned it will grow to five or six feet and become a lovely background or foundation plant, but it can easily be

cut to sixteen or eighteen inches for a superb and truly unusual ground cover.

It not only has shiny leaves which turn bronze-purple in the autumn, but it also has abundant and fragrant white flowers in the spring which arch gracefully, and keep beautifully in flower arrangements. The whole plant has an elegant look to it.

It does best in a moist, acid soil rich with humus. To propagate, place a small stone on top of a low branch. It will root at the spot where it touches the ground.

For an unusual touch, this is my number one choice as an evergreen ground cover, and it has the added advantage of doing equally well in shade or sun. It is hardy as far north as Boston.

Euonymus or Wintercreeper, *Euonymus fortunei,* *Euonymus fortunei coloratus*

Euonymus is often called purple wintercreeper because the green leaves of this vining plant turn a purply-red in the autumn. Because of its clinging habit it has many uses. It will climb upon old stumps, over gates, down banks, or up a house wall. It is a fine ground cover because it roots easily, wherever its vines come into contact with moist soil. However, it tends to have a straggly look unless it is trimmed regularly. When trimming the plant to make a

neat edge, cut the tips five or six inches long. They can be rooted easily.

E. fortunei has leaves from one-half to two inches long.
E. fortunei coloratus has leaves which are *all* about one inch long.

Be wary of euonymus scale which causes the leaves to drop off and the vines to die. Use a systemic insecticide containing Systox, DiSyston or Meta-Syetox R. The plant is hardy as far north as Massachusetts.

Ivy, *Hedera helix, Hedera canariensis*

Ivy is such a useful, adaptable, and cooperative plant for indoor or outdoor use that I wrote a whole book about it, *The Ivy Book, The Growing and Care of Ivy and Ivy Topiary* (Macmillan, 1974, 164 pages). As a ground cover it has everything one could want. It is evergreen and spreads rapidly. It lies flat on the ground, and will climb up banks or down slopes. It prevents soil erosion, grows well under trees, and can be trained into any shape. There are varieties with either all-green or variegated foliage. It will do well in shade, part shade, or sun. It grows faster but is less bushy in the shade because the vines stretch out to seek more light.

It is easy to propagate by taking a cutting about six inches long from the tip of a vine, and rooting it in a mixture of vermicu-

lite and perlite. It is even easier to propagate by "layering." It needs little maintenance, and when you do cut it back to keep a neat shape, you can make cuttings from the clipped ends.

Its only drawback is that it can't be walked on comfortably, but depending on where you plant it, even that can be an advantage. Ideally ivy should be grown in a rich loam which is kept fairly moist.

There are over 200 different varieties of ivy. You can choose any one if you live in an area without frost. The colder your climate is, the more limited your choice becomes. For really cold climates (as far north as Maine) choose from English ivy, Irish ivy, '238th Street' Baltic ivy, or 'Pittsburgh' ivy. For slightly warmer areas like New York City, "Manda's Crested' (my personal favorite) or 'Goldheart' can be added to the selection. In southern California *Hedera canariensis* grows so well it is used by the Department of Highways as a roadside plant.

The American Ivy Society has a research center which grows almost all of the 200 cultivars. For a small membership fee they will answer any query and suggest ivy cultivars which will do well in your area:

> The American Ivy Society
> National Center for American Horticulture
> Mount Vernon, Virginia 22121
> Dues: $7.50 per annum

Ivy, in its adult stage, will fruit and flower.

Pachysandra

Japanese Spurge, *Pachysandra terminalis*

Pachysandra is one of the best of all ground covers for both full shade, and under trees where the competition from tree roots for nourishment makes it hard to grow anything else. Unfortunately, it is also one of the best known ground covers, so if you are striving for the unusual it is a plant to avoid. However, it deserves its popularity. It has a rich green color, a neat habit of growth, and is about ten to twelve inches high. It also spreads rapidly, is evergreen, and even blooms in the spring.

To give your pachysandra bed a different look, try growing it in contained areas under shady trees. I once outlined three circles of ten feet, seven feet, and four feet, with redwood strips and planted pachysandra inside the circles. Between the circles I used black plastic to inhibit weed growth and covered it with white pebbles. The whole effect was pleasing, and a little more unusual than just another great bed of pachysandra.

Because it spreads rapidly with strong underground runners called stolons, be prepared for it to stray into other beds or plantings. It is so aggressive that it can easily take over adjoining areas

Versatile pachysandra can transform a straggly, grassy area into a neat, attractive ring.

unless you cut the runners. If you pull out a runner you may find it to be ten or fifteen feet long with plants growing every few inches.

Although it is simple to propagate by cuttings, it is even easier to lay one of these long runners in a shallow trench two to three inches deep, and cover the runner between the plants with soil.

Don't be tempted to plant spring bulbs amongst pachysandra even though, with no leaves on the trees, there is plenty of light and sun for the bulbs. The strong roots will eventually choke out your bulbs. When the leaves fall from the trees in the autumn, don't rake them out of the pachysandra bed. Let them stay there— they won't blow away because they will be trapped by the thick growth, and by the following spring they will have broken down and become a nourishing mulch for your bed.

Pachysandra does not do well in the sun. It is hardy as far north as New York and Michigan.

Myrtle or Periwinkle, *Vinca minor*

Vinca minor, which is more commonly known as myrtle or periwinkle, is an excellent trailing ground cover in the shade. It is a strong grower without being invasive, and you can safely plant bulbs in its midst without fear of them being strangled. The myrtle foliage will hide the bulb foliage when it begins to wither.

Its leaves, which are about one inch long, are a rich green. It has attractive blue flowers (remember periwinkle blue) about one inch in diameter, and it blooms in the spring. There are several varieties, and they can be distinguished by the color of their flowers; *alba* has white flowers, *atropurpurea* has purple flowers, and *multiplex* has double purple flowers.

If the area you wish to cover gets both shade and sun, myrtle is an excellent choice because it will do equally well in either condition, although in full sun the leaves tend to yellow. It is hardy north to New York and Michigan.

Oregon Holly Grape, *Mahonia aquifolium, Mahonia repens*

I have included mahonia among the evergreen ground covers for it is evergreen in most areas of the United States.

Mahonia aquifolium is a relatively tall grower—about two to three feet—with shiny, dark-green leaves which make a thick covering quite rapidly as it spreads by underground runners. It has small yellow flowers in the spring, followed by tiny blue berries. It withstands very dense shade. Trim it regularly to keep it low and full.

Mahonia repens known as creeping mahonia or dwarf holly grape is a smaller version which grows from eight to ten inches high and has black berries.

Given some protection, both are hardy as far north as New York and Michigan.

Pachistima, *Paxistima canbyi*

Pachistima is a ground cover which grows about one foot high. It becomes so thick it can be clipped into a low hedge, making it an interesting selection for use in bordering other shade plants or to encircle a tree at its outer edge. Its leaves, which are about one inch long and quite narrow, turn an attractive bronze color in the autumn. It has red flowers which bloom in the spring, but they are so tiny they are not a factor to be considered in choosing this plant as a ground cover.

I make a mental note to make cuttings on or about July Fourth so that the new growth will be semi-hard. It is hardy as far north as Massachusetts.

Small Himalayan Sarcococca, *Sarcococca hookeriana humilis*

Small Himalayan sarcococca is a shrub which can grow from one to four feet high, but can easily be cut back so that it becomes a useful ground cover. Cutting it will give the plant a fuller look

Small Himalayan Sarcococca can be used as a ground cover.

and will provide a wealth of cuttings. This is very useful because it
is not an easy plant to find at most nurseries.

It is a good-looking evergreen with glossy foliage. It has fragrant, small white flowers in the spring and black berries in the
fall. It is hardy as far north as Connecticut.

Stonecrop, *Sedum acre, Sedum album*

Although sedum is generally considered a sun-loving plant, it
does grow in dense shade, but it will have fewer flowers and its
foliage will be less compact. It forms large, evergreen, creeping
mats which need little care, and it has tiny succulent leaves about
one-quarter-inch long. It looks well wedged in rock crevices, but
do not use it between steppingstones as the juicy leaves mash easily.

It gets its name from the Latin word *Sedo* (to sit) referring
to its method of creeping on rocks and over the ground. *Sedum
acre* has bright yellow flowers. *Sedum album* has white flowers.
Both are hardy as far north as New York and Michigan.

HERBACEOUS GROUND COVERS

Barren Strawberry, *Waldstenia fragarioides*

For an unusual, very low-growing plant, barren strawberry is worth trying if you have dry soil. It grows only three to four inches high and its glossy one-to-two-inch leaves are like its relative, the strawberry, but it does not bear any fruit as its name indicates. It is most useful on a bank since it grows by a creeping rootstock which helps to retain the soil. In the spring it has little yellow flowers. It is hardy as far north as Connecticut.

Five-leaf Akebia, *Akebia quinata*

If you have a large area which you wish to cover quickly, try akebia. It is not a particularly beautiful plant, or tidy in its growth habit, but it spreads from five to ten feet a year and in some situations that is so great a blessing that many of its faults can be overlooked. But be warned. The plant is such a strong grower that it will take over everything if you are not careful. It will not only climb over walls, stumps, shrubs, and small trees, but will kill any vegetation under it with its smothering growth. Only plant it if you're desperate.

It has tiny, fragrant, purple flowers and leaves shaped like a hand. In the autumn there are pods about three inches long. Propagate by root cuttings or division. It is hardy as far north as Michigan and Vermont.

Bishop's-hat or Barrenwort, *Epimedium*

Epimedium is an exceptionally choice six-to-ten-inch plant that you don't see in every suburban garden although it has been around for a long time. It got its name from Dioscorides, a first century botanist, and it was retained by the famed Swedish botanist Linnaeus (1707–1778).

It has unusually handsome green foliage which turns bronze in the autumn. In the spring it has showy bicolored clusters of delicately-formed, spurred flowers which resemble a small bishop's hat. The flowers are attractive in floral arrangements.

Once it is established, the leaves grow in such dense profusion that even weeds have trouble growing through it. It is such a strong grower that it does well even under a maple tree where shade is dense and competition from roots is great. This is because it grows from a rhizome very near to the surface of the ground. In the autumn you can propagate the plant by dividing the rhizomes.

Epimediums prefer woodland soil, rich with humus or leaf mold, but the real key to keeping it beautiful is to keep it moist. If you don't, you may find that the underfoliage will dry out, encouraging mice, chipmunks or squirrels to nest there. All species are hardy as far north as New York and Michigan.

E. grandiflorum is one of the best species. It has heart-shaped
leaves and white, yellow, or violet flowers.

E. alpinum rubrum has shield-shaped leaves with rose-purple flowers.

E. pinnatum has leaves which are more deeply cut than the others,
and sunshine-yellow flowers.

E. sulphureum has heart-shaped leaves and showy clusters of
sulphur-yellow flowers.

Bugle, *Ajuga reptans*

Bugle, more often called by its botanical name *Ajuga*, is a low-
growing ground cover about four inches high. Its blue flowers come
out in the spring and stand up on six-inch spikes.

It is popular because it spreads rapidly, forms a thick carpet,
and is nearly evergreen. New plants spread by underground runners. It is easy to cut off a runner for planting elsewhere in the garden. It is not a plant I would choose for a large area because it
tends to die out in spots, detracting from a full, lush effect. However, it looks great tucked in among rocks, beside steppingstones,
as a foreground edging plant, or as a ground cover for lilies. For
my taste the leaves are a little too bronzy in color when used as
a ground cover, but look lovely when seen against rocks.

It does best in the shade, but also grows well in the sun. It is
hardy as far north as Michigan and Vermont.

There are many varieties:

A. variegata has leaves edged and splashed with creamy yellow.
A. atropurpurea has bronze leaves.
A. '*Rainbow*' has leaves marbled with dark-red and purple.
A. genevensis has light-green leaves and dark-blue flowers.
A pyramidalis has green foliage, light-blue flowers, and does not spread rapidly.
A. reptans '*Burgundy Glow*' has tricolor leaves.
A. reptans '*Silver Beauty*' has variegated dark-green and cream leaves.

Crested Iris, *Iris cristata* (see also Chapter 3, page 40)

If you want a ground cover with exotic spring flowers which look like small orchids, try crested iris. The flowers, which come in many colors, get their name from the Greek word *Iris* meaning "rainbow," which is descriptive of the plant's many colors.

It has flat, sword-like, four-to-five-inch leaves which creep along the ground fairly rapidly and form a thick mat. I planted mine along a bank on a hillside rockery, and the creeping rhizomes did a first-class job of preventing soil erosion caused by heavy rains in the spring.

Keep the plant fairly moist in well-drained soil, but do not plant too deeply or mulch too heavily or it may rot. The plant disappears in mid-autumn, but remembering those lovely little flowers will help you forget this disadvantage. It is hardy as far north as Wisconsin, Vermont, and Maine.

Galax, *Galax aphylla*

I have described galax quite completely in the chapter on woodland gardens (p. 54). Don't overlook galax as a ground cover in a cultivated garden. It is effective planted in front of azaleas or used as an edging for a shady border. Don't forget to give it moist soil enriched with humus. It is hardy to Wisconsin, Vermont, and Maine.

Galax

Goutweed, *Aegopodium podagraria*

Goutweed is such a strong grower that it should be used only in desperation where you want a sturdy quick cover that will really take over. I include it here because some areas require just such an invasive grower. It will grow anywhere—shade or sun, good soil

or poor. It will even grow under maple trees where little else will. But be warned, it can become a weed. It can even be mowed once or twice a year to keep it low and in check.

It grows about eight to twelve inches high and has an uninteresting white flower in the spring. Its leaves and roots were supposedly used as a remedy for gout in medieval Europe. There is a variegated variety, *Aegopodium podograria variegatum,* that has attractive white-edged leaves.

Ground Ivy, *Nepeta hederacea*

Ground ivy (which is not a true ivy) is a creeping plant which can be used effectively between steppingstones because it not only

lies flat, but can be stepped on without harm. I once used it very satisfactorily on the bank of a river where I could not use grass and wanted something green. Pity it doesn't stay green all year for it truly "grows like a weed."

Plant it in moist soil where you want something to "take over" and you will bless it. Plant in a restricted area and you will curse it. It is hardy as far north as New York and Vermont.

Hosta

Hostas could have been discussed in the chapter on ground covers or the chapter on flowering perennials. They are superb shade plants, magnificent as ground covers, and equally sensational as fragrant, blooming perennial flowers. There is such variation in leaf shape and size that whole areas can be planted in a shade garden with remarkable effect.

It is one of those few plants that almost requires no care. Once you get a good clump going, you have little to do but sit back and admire it. They stand erect without staking and they rarely need to be sprayed. And every few years they can be divided so that you have many more plants. I once used the division of hostas as an object lesson for a teen-ager in just how little a garden need cost if you are willing to put in just a little effort. We bought five hostas (*H. undulata media picta*) at one dollar apiece at a local discount garden center. We planted them together in the shade at Candle-

wood Lake, Connecticut. The following year the plants were large
enough to be divided into two or three plants and we had thirteen.
The next year we had thirty and after that seventy! Today it is a
large, lush, cool oasis—all for only five dollars.

You may have heard hosta called plantain lily or funkia. These
names have been used at one time or another by horticulturists,
but the correct nomenclature is hosta.

Hosta's leaf shapes vary from heart-shaped to elongated ovals,
and their leaves are from two to eight inches wide, and from four
to eighteen inches long. Some are all green or blue-green, others
are variegated green with white edges, or creamy-white streaked
with green. Flowers range from pure white to lavender, purple, or
blue. Some are so fragrant they perfume a whole garden.

Hostas grow best in a well-drained, humus-rich soil, but do
well in almost any soil so long as it is kept moist. The only disadvantage hosta has is that it completely dies down in the winter,
leaving the soil bare; but each spring when the new leaves come
up looking so beautifully fresh and clean I forget about the bare
spot I had.

H. albo marginata has stunning large leaves edged with a broad
band of white, and lavender flowers in September.

H. caerulea lanceolata has broad, lustrous, green leaves. In July
and August it has blue flowers.

H. fortunei aurea marmorata has green leaves mottled with yellow
in broad patches. Flowers are produced just above the leaves.

H. fortunei robusta is a giant hosta often reaching a height of five
or six feet. It has large, broad leaves and pale-lilac flowers in
midsummer.

H. japonica blue is a fast grower, extremely hardy, and in midsummer is covered with blue flowers.

H. sieboldiana has large blue-green leaves. Don't fertilize it if you
want the leaves to remain blue-green.

H. subcordata grandiflora has very fragrant, large, pure-white, lily-
shaped flowers which bloom throughout August and September.
It is one of my favorites.

H. undulata media picta is the kind you see most often as a ground
cover because it rapidly forms a solid bed. It has green or
variegated foliage and lavender flowers. It is extremely hardy.

H. ventricosa has blue leaves and unusually handsome blue flowers
which grow eighteen inches tall and are ideal for cut flowers.

There are some new miniatures but these are hard to locate at nurseries. If you are making a collection and want more information about hostas, write to:

The American Hosta Society
114 The Fairway
Albert Lea, Minnesota 56007
Dues: $5.00 per annum

Lily of the Valley, *Convallaria majalis*

Lily of the valley is known as the flower for lovers, and in France on May 1 it is the custom to give a little bunch to the person you love. The sidewalk cafes in Paris are heavy with its sweet, scented perfume on that date. In French it is called *muquet*. It gets its botanical name from the Latin *convallis* (valley) which refers to its native place of growth.

Although it is usually thought of as an accent plant grown in little clusters in a rock or woodland garden, when it is planted closely together it becomes a delightful ground cover. It has a disadvantage, of course, in that it cannot be walked upon without being crushed, and it disappears with the first frost.

It has two, oval, six-to-eight-inch, green leaves and fragrant, bell-like flowers grow on a stem between these leaves in the spring. The plants increase rapidly, and dividing the plants every few years will not only give you more plants, but each one will bloom better.

Plant it in moist soil, enriched with fertilizer and humus, and under deciduous trees where it will get light in the spring, and it will do well for you. Plant it under an evergreen tree and blooms may be sparse. It is subject to spider mites so watch out for tiny white speckling on the leaves which will tip you off that mites are at work. If so, spray with Malathion. It is hardy as far north as Maine.

Lilyturf, *Liriope muscari*

If you can provide lilyturf (which is not a lily) with strong light by pruning or thinning the trees which shade it, you will find it to be an interesting ground cover or accent plant. Growing from twelve-inch clumps, it has bold, narrow, lily-like green or variegated leaves, and an interesting white or lilac flower which grows on an upright stalk late in the summer. The foliage resembles the popular "spider" houseplant.

Although the foliage turns pale in autumn, the leaves do not completely disappear and leave your ground bare. It does not do well much further north than New York City.

Lilyturf

Ribbon grass or Gardener's-garters, *Phalaris arundinacea picta*

Ribbon grass is a handsome, wild-looking, tall grass which looks well in the garden because of its two-to-three-foot-long, slender leaves which are striped longitudinally and are excellent for use in flower arrangements. Although the leaves die in the winter, they remain erect and do not create a bare look.

Care must be taken, however, to keep it in bounds because it is a rapid grower and spreads by underground stolens. It grows in poor dry soil.

Its name *Phalaris* is the old Greek word for grass. It is hardy to Michigan and Vermont.

Spotted Dead Nettle, *Lamium maculatum*

Let me start by saying I particularly like Lamium even though many other gardeners avoid it because of its rapid growth. One "expert" described it as "extremely weedy and unworthy of a place even in the wild garden." Well, perhaps she never had a garden with a large shady area that needed a low-growing, pretty-leaved plant which would cover the bare ground quickly. For this purpose, Lamium (I don't like its common name spotted dead nettle) is ideal.

This lovely, albeit invasive plant has beautiful 1½-inch, silver and green, serrated, heart-shaped leaves which grow on stems no more than six inches high, and spread out in all directions from little clumps. It isn't even fussy about soil. Unworthy? Humph! It is hardy as far north as New York and Michigan.

Sweet Woodruff

Sweet Woodruff, *Asperula odorata*

Sweet woodruff is a perfectly charming ground cover with lots of dividends. The foliage is not only aromatic, but pretty with its whorls of one-inch leaves on six-inch stems. It is used as the flavoring agent for May wine and snips of it are delicious in any punch. I even use it in Sangria or Pimms' Cup.

It is a perfect companion plant for small bulbs, for edging a border, or under rhododendrons or azaleas. It should be kept quite moist. It is hardy as far north as Michigan and Vermont.

Yellowroot, *Xanthorhiza simplicissima*

Yellowroot is a tidy-looking, easy-to-care-for plant which is useful in areas where you need a two-foot uniform growth. It has dainty purple flowers in nodding sprays which appear before the leaves. The leaves are one to two inches long and turn a warm yellow in the autumn. Its bark and roots are also yellow, hence its name.

It grows rapidly but must be provided with moist soil. It grows well at the edge of a pond. It is hardy as far north as New York and Vermont.

6

❁❁❁❁❁❁❁❁❁❁

Shrubs— Misunderstood, Misused, Misplaced Treasures...

Shrubs somehow have never received the consideration and respect that they are entitled to. The way they are planted in so many gardens, with so little imagination used in their selection, leads me to believe that people do not realize their value and have no idea of the many useful purposes they serve. Shrubs can do so much for a garden and they can do it faster than trees. They can enclose our gardens and our properties with hedges of living green. They can offer dramatic backgrounds for flowers. They can screen out unpleasant sights and provide us with a permanently pleasant one. They can soften harsh lines of land or buildings. They can provide magnificent and often fragrant bloom from spring through summer. They can offer food and shelter for birds during winter. And they do it all with just a little care and attention . . . and permanently.

Years ago, the list of shrubs offered in nurseries was limited, but that is no longer the case. Now we can get shrubs from all over the world to fit practically any location or situation. There is no longer any excuse for the limited variety of shrubs found in many gardens. Today there are so many truly exotic and exciting modern shrubs that you can have as much fun in the choosing as in the growing. All you need to keep in mind is the effect you want to create. It is much easier to remedy existing garden conditions to meet the soil and light requirements of a desired shrub, than to go without that shrub.

The thirty-five shrubs listed here will grow in areas with strong light, and with at least two to three hours of sunlight each day. There's no difficulty in finding plenty of shrubs to grow in the shade —some evergreen, others deciduous, some with beautiful flowers, others with lush foliage, and some with both.

High on my list of favorite evergreen shrubs is andromeda with its lustrous, ever-glistening leaves and lily of the valley-type flowers. Leucothoë, if you prune it correctly (see p. 106), is fabulous as a shrub, and does equally well as a flowering perennial or ground cover. Skimmia, a lush, low shrub with bright-red berries is another beauty. And of course, rhododendrons and azaleas give you literally thousands of species and varieties to choose from. The deciduous shrubs I find interesting in the shade are: Alabama fothergilla with flowers like white bottle brushes; the fringe tree with masses of feathery, white, fringed, fragrant flowers; kerria with bright-yellow, buttercup-type flowers; and clethra with flowers so fragrant they can perfume a whole garden.

You can really have fun with your shrub collection and meet other interested people by joining the many plant societies devoted to shade-loving shrubs, such as the Rhododendron, Holly, or Camellia Societies. (Addresses on p. 213.) They will keep you up to date on all the new varieties and hybrids. Once you start your collection, carefully label your plants with name, date of planting, color, etc. Other society members will be interested in your experiences.

The old saw about digging a ten-dollar hole for a one-dollar plant never applied as well as it does with shrubs—particularly those grown in the shade. Shade soil is usually hard, dry, airless, and just plain poor. Dig your shrub hole deep and then mix plenty of builder's-type sand (not the seaside variety), some humus (peat, leaf mold, or compost), and some food (manure, bone meal, dried blood or slow-release chemicals). After your shrub is in the ground, put a mulch on top of the soil. It will not only help retain moisture, but will eliminate the need for constant weeding. One word of caution—be careful about using peat moss as a mulch. It often cakes and prevents moisture from entering the soil. Try not to walk on shrub beds under trees lest you pack the soil and form a crust. Then neither air nor water can get in.

The United States Department of Agriculture issues a little pamphlet called *Selecting Shrubs for Shady Areas,* and a very good one it is, too.* Some of its advice is worth noting here.

Many kinds of shrubs are easy to grow in shady areas, and once established they require little care. Regular watering during dry periods and some fertilizing during the growing season will satisfy the needs of most shrubs.

To grow shrubs in shade areas—

Start with nursery-grown stock adapted to your area.

Plant during late winter or early spring in well-prepared soil.

Maintain a mulch around them.

Water regularly.

When you select a shrub, consider whether you want to—

Beautify an area by planting masses of colorful flowers, berries, or foliage.

Screen a particular view

Accent the lines of a building.

Some shrubs, the low ones, are best used for ground covers or borders; some, the tall ones are best used for screens; and some, the colorful ones, are best used for ornamental groupings. Before selecting a shrub for your garden, make sure it will grow well in your hardiness zone. Hardiness is the plant's tolerance to high or low temperatures. Other factors such as wind velocity, soil conditions, humidity and availability of moisture also play an important role.

Visit local gardens—see what grows well in your area. You can get advice about selecting shrubs from your nurseryman, County Agricultural Agent, or State Extension Horticulturist.

Shrubs growing wild in the woods are generally harder to transplant and need more initial care than shrubs you buy from a nursery.

There's a whole new world out there for you once you start getting interested in nature's great treasures—shrubs. Enjoy them.

* *Home and Garden Bulletin* No. 142, United States National Arboretum Agricultural Research Service, Washington, D.C., revised September 1974 (thirty cents)

DECIDUOUS SHRUBS

Alabama Fothergilla, *Fothergilla monticola, Fothergilla gardenii*

For an unusual accent, Alabama fothergilla offers an attractive outline. It grows from six to eight feet tall in an upright spreading mound. In the spring it has fragrant flowers on the ends of its branches which look like white bottle brushes. The plant has attractive one-to-two-inch, deeply veined, bright-green leaves which turn yellow and red in the fall.

Grow it in slightly acid soil which is sufficiently porous for good drainage, but has sufficient humus to retain moisture.

Dwarf fothergilla (*F. gardenii*) grows no more than three to four feet high and makes an effective border or woodland plant.

It is native from Virginia to Alabama, but is hardy as far north as Philadelphia.

Alabama Fothergilla

Bayberry, *Myrica pensylvanica*

Bayberry is an upright ten-to-twelve-foot shrub with many small twigs, and two-to-four-inch, egg-shaped, dull-green leaves. It also has very fragrant, light-gray, waxy berries which hang onto the branches throughout the winter, long after the leaves have gone. These are the berries that early Massachusetts settlers boiled to make candles, and which are now so prized at Christmastime.

Bayberry prefers a sandy, dry, acid soil, and is easily grown along the coast where it is useful as a windbreak or shield against shifting sand. Given the same sandy acid soil it grows as well inland. It is hardy throughout New England.

Bush Honysuckle, *Diervilla sessilifolia*

If you've seen weigela you know what bush honeysuckle looks like. It grows about four feet high and has graceful arching branches. In the spring lovely yellow flowers grow in clusters along the stem. The cut, flowering branches look beautiful in floral arrangements.

It should be allowed to grow naturally so that it shows off its fountain-like branches. It is sad to see this charming plant cut back to a rigid form. It is an easy plant to grow, asking little more than good garden soil to which peat or compost has been added at planting time. It is hardy as far north as New York and Michigan.

Cutleaf Stephanandra, *Stephanandra incisa*

Stephanandra is a little shrub which rarely grows more than three to four feet high and has exceptionally lovely 2½-inch, fern-like leaves which turn orange-red in the autumn. In spring it has delicate, greenish-white blossoms. It is mainly grown for its appealing foliage. It makes a lovely border plant, and even though it loses its leaves in winter, its slender, bright-brown branches arch so gracefully it remains attractive throughout the winter.

It is an easy plant to grow, requiring only well-drained, good garden soil to which some humus has been added. It is hardy to New York and Michigan.

Cutleaf Stephanandra

False Spirea, *Sorbaria sorbifolia*

False spirea is like its relative spirea, but it is a more upright plant about five to eight feet tall with plumes of creamy-white, twelve-to-eighteen-inch flowers from summer to fall. The foliage,

which resembles mountain ash, is fern-like and very handsome. It looks particularly well in a mass planting where the flowers can make a dramatic showing.

False spirea is easy to grow and likes a good garden soil that is kept moist. It is hardy north to Connecticut.

Five-leaf Aralia, *Acanthopanax sieboldianus*

Five-leaf aralia is a rugged, tough, eight-foot-tall plant able to withstand a great deal of abuse. It even thrives in big city gardens where it has to fight soot, gases, and other pollutants. It has shiny, deep-green leaves which resemble Virginia creeper, and because it creates a dense mass of foliage on arching branches it is most useful as a background plant or screen. The leaves are attractive in flower arrangements too.

It is not fussy about soil or moisture, and can be counted on to look fresh when others are suffering from drought. It loses its leaves in the winter, and is hardy as far north as Boston.

Forsythia

In New York, I know that spring, my favorite season, is at hand when the forsythia blooms and its arched branches are covered with sunny, yellow blossoms. I feel like a child let out of school and I'm ready to don my knee pads and garden gloves and get to work. It grieves me to see this plant, which has such natural grace, sheared back into rigid shapes even though it does make a good hedge with compact masses of leaves. That clever gardener and editor, Marjorie J. Dietz, suggests using forsythia as an espalier, and this idea is sufficiently interesting that I would be willing to train my long graceful branches.

The bell-like flowers remain on the branches for about three weeks before the green leaves appear. Branches cut late in winter or in very early spring will easily bloom indoors. Forsythia will bloom in the shade, but not as profusely as in the sun.

F. 'Beatrix Farrand' is a vigorous grower, reaching six to eight feet. It has immense flowers that are frequently two inches in diameter. This forsythia, which is very hardy, originated in the Arnold Arboretum in Boston where it was named for Beatrix Farrand, one of America's foremost woman landscape architects.

F. 'Lynwood Gold' grows from five to seven feet tall. It has superb deep-yellow flowers on erect branches and blooms in a most profuse manner.

F. 'Spring Glory' grows from six to nine feet tall. It has pale-yellow flowers which cover the branches in such masses that they literally bend from the weight.

Fringe Tree, *Chionanthus virginicus*

Fringe tree is such a lovely shrub that it is worth trying to grow it in the shade. As long as you can provide some broken sunlight as well as strong light, you should have success with it.

In the late spring the tree is covered with masses of fringed, white, fragrant flowers hanging from large lustrous leaves. There are male and female plants and although the male flowers are larger, both have lovely flowers. If you wish to have the extra dividend of blue berries in the autumn, you must have at least one of each sex. Since the fringe tree is a large shrub, growing from fifteen to twenty feet tall, it makes a good accent, corner, or background plant.

It is not fussy about soil as long as it is kept moist. It grows naturally along river banks in the south. It is hardy as far north as New York City if planted in a protected position.

Fringe Tree

Jetbead, *Rhodotypos scandens*

Jetbead is a four-to-five-foot, spreading shrub with bright-green foliage and a graceful, airy look. It has two-inch, white, four-petaled flowers which begin to bloom in the spring and keep opening throughout the summer. In the autumn it has shiny black seeds which give the plant its common name.

It is a tough little plant, tolerant of city pollution and arid soil as well as shade. Prune it in the early spring to keep it full and bushy. It is hardy to Boston.

Kerria, *Kerria japonica*

Kerria is a dainty little plant which rarely grows more than three or four feet high and has slender, bright-green, arching stems. In the spring it is covered with single or double bright-yellow, buttercup-type flowers. Its long tapering leaves are darker on top than on the undersurface. It is not a plant for a bold accent, but should be used to soften a line or hide ungainly stalks of other shrubs whose foliage does not begin for several feet. Planted near perennials or spring bulbs it effectively hides dying foliage. It is hardy throughout most of the United States.

Kerria

Korean Abelia-leaf, *Abeliophyllum distichum*

The Korean abelia-leaf resembles its near-relative, the forsythia, except that it is much smaller—not more than three or four feet in height—and is a slow grower. It has white, fragrant, bell-shaped flowers which bloom in the early spring before its blue-green, pointed leaves appear. It is sometimes called white forsythia, and like forsythia can be cut to hasten growth in late winter.

Try to plant it in a protected location because its flower buds can be damaged by late spring frosts. It is not too fussy about soil so long as it is well-drained. It is hardy as far north as Boston.

Korean Abelia-leaf

Oakleaf Hydrangea, *Hydrangea quercifolia*

The hydrangea in its many species is a popular flowering shrub commonly seen throughout America. But the oakleaf hydrangea not only withstands shade better than the others, it also has the most beautiful oak-like leaves which form a mass of rich-green foliage that turns red and purple in autumn. Its white flowers are more lacy than other species and turn from pink to rose as they fade.

It grows about five feet tall, needs little pruning, and looks well in cultivated or woodland gardens. It is hardy north to New York and Michigan.

Oakleaf Hydrangea

Red Chokeberry, *Aronia arbutifolia*

Red chokeberry is a charming plant in the springtime with its clusters of small white flowers which resemble apple blossoms, but it is in the autumn that it comes into its glory. Then its foliage turns a brilliant scarlet, and its branches are dotted with red berries which remain all winter even after the leaves are gone.

It will grow well in most soils so long as it is kept moist. It is an excellent choice for planting beside a pond or swamp. It is hardy as far north as Boston.

Snowberry, *Symphoricarpos albus*

Snowberry is a four-to-six-foot shrub which does exceedingly well in heavy shade, and makes an interesting border plant in an area where little else will grow. Although it has tiny pink flowers in summer, it is grown mainly for its large, white, juicy berries in the autumn.

It is a strong grower and does well in almost any soil. It is hardy throughout the United States.

Snowberry

Spicebush, *Lindera benzoin*

Spicebush is a native, upright shrub that grows from ten to fifteen feet tall and has dense clusters of small, yellow, button-like, fuzzy flowers which appear very early in the spring—even before forsythia. It has bright-green, three-to-five-inch, oval leaves which turn yellow in autumn when the branches are studded with bunches of scarlet berries. Early American settlers used its leaves and bark for making tea and medicine.

It is found wild in woodlands and swamps along the eastern seaboard, south to Virginia. In the cultivated garden it should be grown in good garden soil enriched with leaf mold and kept moist.

Spicebush

Summer Sweet or Sweet Pepper Bush, *Clethra alnifolia*

Summer sweet is an eight-foot shrub with three-inch, shiny, bright-green leaves and abundant, four-to-six-inch spikes of long-lasting white or pink flowers. The flowers are good for cutting, but the shrub's main advantage is its spicy fragrance which can perfume a whole garden. It is heavenly!

It has two requirements; rich, peaty, acid soil, and plenty of moisture. Plant it near azaleas and rhododendrons because they all like the same conditions. If your shade is too dense the plant will get lanky. It is hardy as far north as Boston.

Winter Hazel, *Corylopsis spicata, Corylopsis pauciflora, Corylopsis sinensis*

Winter hazel has pretty, five-petaled, yellow flowers which bloom very early in the spring on the bare twigs of the plant. You'll see their clusters of flowers about the same time as the forsythia. They have distinctive heart-shaped leaves from two to five inches long, depending on the specie. They are hardy as far north as New York and Michigan.

C. spicata grows from four to six feet high and nearly as wide.
C. pauciflora is a smaller version of *C. spicata,* grows from three
   to five feet high, and has dense, delicately-pleated leaves.
C. sinensis grows about six feet high and has leaves with a bluish
   cast.

Winter Hazel

Witch Hazel, *Hamamelis Virginiana*

The witch hazel, unlike so many other shrubs, blooms in the early fall when it has showy, bright-yellow flowers with four petals. After the flower has bloomed a seed pod develops, and when it is fully ripe it explosively discharges two black seeds. Witch hazel

grows from eight to fifteen feet tall and prefers cool, damp soil. It is hardy throughout America.

EVERGREEN SHRUBS

Japanese Andromeda, *Pieris japonica*

Andromeda is an outstanding shrub by any set of standards. Its shape is neat, upright, and graceful. Its three-inch-long, spreading clusters of leaves are evergreen, lustrous, and glossy. Its flowers, which resemble cascades of lilies of the valley, are showy and dramatic. Even the flower buds, which appear in winter, are interesting because they are made up of clusters of many tight, tiny buds.

It is a particularly important foundation plant because it grows about six feet high and is a continuous performer throughout every season. Because it grows so gracefully it looks equally well in a woodland setting. I grew mine beside a waterfall in Connecticut where the pendulous white tassels looked very dramatic against the rocks.

It requires acid soil. When planting, add plenty of peat, leaf mold, or compost and keep it moist. It is hardy north to Boston.

Barberry, *Berberis thunbergii, Berberis verruculosa*

The barberry grows from four to six feet tall and has extremely dense branches covered with little, one-inch leaves which turn red or yellow in the autumn. Its tiny, yellow, spring flowers are followed by red or black berries. Some species listed below are deciduous, others are evergreen.

It is an easy plant to grow in ordinary garden soil and will even withstand the rigors of a city garden. You don't even have to be attentive to watering if you add some humus, peat, or compost when you first plant it.

There are several reasons why I like barberry in spite of its overuse: Its dense thorny growth makes it a sensational screen for keeping unwanted animals, children, or people (not necessarily in that order) out of your garden, without the obvious use of a fence. The growth is so thick and compact that it lends itself to topiary cutting in interesting shapes or forms, and can therefore be used

in strategic places in the garden as an accent note. The fall coloring is striking. The leaves turn a brilliant scarlet and the berries stay on the branches throughout the winter. If you like to experiment with your artistic talents, vigorous pruning and cutting will give it a Japanese bonsai-like form. Wear heavy gloves however; those thorns have sharp points.

Berberis thunbergii (Japanese barberry) is deciduous, and has yellow flowers, scarlet autumn leaves, and red berries. It is hardy throughout the United States.

Berberis verruculosa (warty barberry) is evergreen, and has attractive, little orange flowers. Its shiny green leaves are almost white underneath and its twigs are warty looking. It is almost as hardy as Japanese barberry, but in colder climates, plant it in a protected position if possible. There is a dwarf variety 'Minor,' which grows only eighteen inches high and is a very slow grower.

Camellia, *Camellia japonica, Camellia sasanqua, Camellia reticulata*

Camellias, with their perfect flowers, always bring the antebellum South, Scarlett O'Hara, and southern belles to mind, and I guess that is logical since that is the area of the United States where they thrive and become such magnificent plants. Even the head-

quarters of the American Camellia Society is in Georgia. There are over 600 named varieties of camellias in a wide range of reds, pinks, and whites. Unlike the gardenia, which they resemble, they have little or no fragrance. They grow usually from six to fifteen feet tall, but in the South they sometimes grow to thirty feet.

In the colder, northern parts of the United States they are hard to grow. Except for *C. sasanqua*, it isn't even worth trying to grow them north of New York City. Even between Philadelphia and New York City, it is an "iffy" proposition unless you can plant them in a position sheltered from prevailing winter winds. But the flowers of this shrub are so fabulously beautiful that it is worth the effort.

Even if you live in an area which doesn't get too cold or windy, there are certain musts for successful growing. The soil *must* be well-drained yet moist. The pH of the soil *must* be between 5.5 and 6.5 (5.5 is better since they are happiest in acid soil). They *must* be shaded from early morning sun (this is one of those times you can be grateful for a shady garden), but they do need *some* sun. In dense shade only minimal flowering will occur.

There are three species of Camellias in general cultivation in the United States.

C. japonica is the species with gorgeous flowers four or five inches wide that are double or semi-double, and sometimes are streaked with two-tone colors. It generally blooms in the early spring, although there are varieties which bloom in the winter. North of Philadelphia, only those varieties which bloom in early spring should be grown. Those blooming in winter will have their blossoms blasted by frost. South of New York City those worth trying are: 'Bernice Boddy,' pink; mathothiana, red; and leucantha, white.

C. sasanqua is much more tolerant of cold than *C. japonica*, but its flower, though lovely, is less showy. It blooms from October to Christmas, and is hardy through Connecticut and Massachusetts. It usually grows from four to seven feet tall and its flowers are pink, white, or red. There are many varieties to choose from. Some nice ones are 'Cleopatra,' rose-pink; 'Crimson Tide,' red; and mine-no-yuki, white.

C. reticulata is the tenderest of the camellias. It blooms in the spring and has very large flowers. It is usually grown outdoors in southern California, but in other areas it needs indoor protection during the winter.

Drooping Leucothoë, *Leucothoë catesbaei*

I have arbitrarily included leucothoë, a shrub, among the ground covers (p. 106) because when cut low it serves that purpose with such elegance and distinction.

I could have also listed it among the flowering perennials because it has such lovely, white, waxy, bell-shaped flowers which bloom in the spring. Left unpruned however, it grows five to six feet and it belongs here with evergreen shrubs. It is a marvelous foundation, border, or woodland plant. For cultivation suggestions refer back to p. 106.

Glossy Abelia, *Abelia grandiflora*

Glossy abelia is most useful in a shade garden because of its versatility. Left untrimmed, its gracefully arching stems with small, 1½-inch, dark-green leaves make a beautiful accent plant with a spread of about six feet. Trimmed, it makes an excellent hedge. It

has clusters of flowers too, which bloom from June until autumn. Pink and faintly fragrant, each blossom is tubular in shape like its relative the honeysuckle, and the sprays make good cut flowers. There are dwarf forms: 'Edward Goucher' and 'Sherwoodi.'

The plant is a better grower south of Philadelphia where it is evergreen. In colder areas it is deciduous. If part dies in winter, cut out all dead wood early in the spring. It is not reliably hardy north of Connecticut. Plant it in well-drained, acid soil to which peat moss and leaf mold have been added.

Heavenly Bamboo, *Nandina domestica*

Heavenly bamboo is a six-to-eight-foot shrub with fern-like, red-green foliage, clusters of large white flowers in midsummer, and bright berries in autumn and winter. Despite its common name, it is not a bamboo, although the foliage is reminiscent of some of the delicately leaved bamboos. It is in the barberry family.

James Bush-Brown, former head of the Department of Landscape Design at the Pennsylvania School of Horticulture, writes in his book, *Shrubs and Trees for the Home Landscape* (Chilton Books), that the plant was named *Nandina domestica* because it is found beside the door in Chinese homes where the plant is native.

It is an age-old custom for a newly married couple to plant a *Nandina* at the door of their home. If there is ever discord in the family the husband and the wife separately will go outside and tell their troubles to the *Nandina*. Thus, with a gentle relief of tension, harmony may be restored to the home.

Nandina should be planted in soil enriched with leaf mold, and kept moist. South of Washington, D.C. it is evergreen, north to New Jersey it is deciduous. In protected areas it is hardy as far north as New York City.

Holly, *Ilex crenata, Ilex glabra, Ilex verticillata*

There are hundreds of species and varieties of holly, many of which do not look anything like the Christmas-card version with sharp, thorny-toothed leaves. Some are evergreen, others deciduous. All, however, have their own genders, and you must have a male and female planted nearby in order to produce berries.

Ilex crenata (Japanese holly) is an upright, evergreen holly which grows from five to fifteen feet tall, and has shiny, dark-green, serrated leaves and small black berries on ascending stems. It is a very robust plant and is one of the few selected by the United States Department of Agriculture as being tolerant of dense shade and city conditions. It is hardy as far north as Connecticut.

Ilex glabra (inkberry) has dark-green, slightly toothed leaves and black berries. It is an upright, slender shrub which grows about seven feet tall in moist soil or even woodland swamp. It grows very slowly and is hardy throughout the United States.

Ilex verticillata (winterberry) is a handsome holly which, although deciduous, has red berries that remain on the branches throughout most of the winter unless the birds eat them. These bare, berried-branches are marvelous in autumn and winter flower arrangements. Winterberry grows in a broad spreading manner up to about ten feet tall and likes moist soil or wet land. It is hardy throughout the United States.

The genus is so large, so complicated, and so interesting that it has its own plant society.

The Holly Society of America, Inc.
407 Fountain Green Road
Bel Air, Maryland 21014
Dues: $5.00 per annum

Japanese Aucuba, *Aucuba japonica*

Don't try to grow Japanese aucuba unless you live south of Maryland; but if you do, it's a great shade shrub. It is a handsome, evergreen, accent plant that grows from six to ten feet tall and has thick, shiny leaves and bright-red berries. Be sure to buy both male and female plants if you want to have berries. Only the female produces the berries, but both sexes must be in the same vicinity before these berries can appear. The plant likes a moist, fertile soil.

Leatherleaf Mahonia, *Mahonia bealii*

Leatherleaf mahonia is not graceful, but planted in the right place, it is very effective because of its striking stiffness. Pruned with an eye to stressing its exotic quality it can be an interesting specimen plant. It grows from eight to twelve feet tall.

All the mahonias (see Chapter 5, page 112) are excellent shade plants, and leatherleaf is no exception, although it is not hardy in areas where the temperature drops below zero. It has large, fragrant, pale-yellow flower clusters on short stems in the spring, and leathery, dark-green leaves. Plant it in a rich, humus-filled soil, feed with bone meal, and keep mulched to retain moisture.

Mountain Laurel, *Kalmia latifolia*

Mountain laurel is a splendid plant for a shade garden. Its evergreen leaves are about four inches long, and in the spring it has round, four-to-five-inch clusters of flowers which are pink in bud and gradually change to white in full flower. To take one single flower from a cluster and examine its perfect form is to be reminded that as an artist, nature has no peer. It was named after the Swedish botanist, Peter Kalm, who first discovered it.

The plant has a compact, bushy form and grows from six to eight feet tall in a cultivated garden. In areas like the Appalachian Mountains, where it is wild, it is often twenty feet tall.

To be successful, mountain laurel must be grown in acid soil which is kept moist. Mix plenty of compost and leaf mold into the soil at the time of planting, and each year add more around the base of the plants as a top dressing so that the soil retains as much moisture as possible. Don't work it into the soil because the plant has shallow roots. Oak leaves are very acid, and make the best leaf mold for mountain laurel. In dense shade the plant is less compact and the flowering is sparser. It is hardy throughout the United States.

Mountain Laurel

Japanese Pittosporum, *Pittosporum tobira*

Pittosporum is a popular shade plant in California and the southern region of the United States. It grows from six to ten feet

tall, has shiny, dark, evergreen leaves, and its flowers have a heady, orange blossom fragrance. It is effective as a single specimen plant, or clipped to form a neat hedge. It grows best in rich garden soil.

Privet, *Ligustrum*

The word "privet" is used so often with "hedge" that it is hard to think of the plant in any other context. But here are many species and varieties which left untrimmed, are effective when used as foundation plants or shrub borders. Although all privets have flowers, they are grown mainly for their leaves. Some are deciduous, others evergreen. All are very sturdy growers, require little care, and can be grown in any good garden soil.

L. obtusifolium is deciduous and is the hardiest of all the privets, surviving even a Montreal winter. It has dense, one-to-two-inch leaves on strong stalks and is a prolific bloomer. Little white flowers appear in mid-June followed by black berries.

L. lucidum is evergreen and hardy as far north as Philadelphia. It has large, glossy leaves from three to five inches long. In midsummer it has white, tubular flowers which grow in clusters on the ends of the branches. Its average height is from six to ten feet, but in the south this "shrub" grows to thirty feet.

L. japonicum is evergreen and hardy as far north as New York City. It has handsome, three-inch, glossy leaves, and four-inch flower clusters in July. It looks particularly charming when left unpruned.

Privet

Rhododendrons and Azaleas

The blooms of the rhododendron and azalea are among the most beautiful and spectacular in the flower world, and the plants rank near the top of any popularity list. It is not possible to deal with them fully on these pages since there are thousands of species, but if you are sufficiently interested, there are many fine books written exclusively about them. I have lumped rhododendrons and azaleas together, not only because they are in the same plant family (an azalea is part of the genus Rhododendron), but because they require the same care and conditions.

Azalea

They are the perfect shrub for foundation planting, borders, or an accent note. (Check your pH regularly if planted near a cement wall.) Whole gardens can be planted with just rhododendrons and azaleas. There are rhododendrons which grow forty feet tall; others are dwarf and never grow higher than twenty-four inches. Some azaleas are exotic when bonsaied, others are graceful when used in a hanging basket. Both are excellent for tub culture. Their colors are as varied as the rainbow—red, rose, and pink; yellow, orange, and salmon; purple, blue, and lavender. All rhododendrons are evergreen. Some azaleas are evergreen, others are deciduous.

They are easy plants to grow as long as you remember these important rules:

1. They must be grown in acid soil.
2. The soil must be kept cool and moist.
3. They must have good drainage.

Use at least fifty percent peat moss, leaf mold, or compost when planting, and add a mulch of leaves (preferably oak) every year. A constant mulch is a key to successful growing because it keeps the soil cool, moist, and nourished. They grow best in a moisture-ladened atmosphere. It's no surprise to find the American Rhododendron Society headquartered in Oregon where the weather is humid for a good part of the year.

I do not want to mislead you about growing rhododendrons and azaleas in the shade. They *do* bloom more profusely in the sun,

Azalea

Rhododendron

but if they get strong light and at least two hours of sun a day, you will have some blooms, and their colors will be even more intense.

Don't cultivate around your plants because their roots are near the surface and will be damaged. When you fertilize, choose one which is especially formulated for acid-loving plants. Do not use an ordinary balanced fertilizer suitable for other garden plants because it will leave an alkaline residue. Organic fertilizers such as cotton-seed meal or fish meal are excellent. So is ammonium sulphate. Hollytone is an excellent commercial fertilizer, as is Ortho's Rhododendron 5–10–10.

Among many gardeners there is a question about removing the old seed heads (called deadheading) from rhododendrons. The answer is categoric—do it. After blooming, carefully remove the old bloom trusses just below the lowest flower. If you have forgotten or failed to do this in the summer or fall, then deadhead the plants in the spring. Failure to get those seed heads off the plant may lead to flowering only every other year. When pruning, cut immediately above a rosette of leaves. The growth buds of rhododendrons are formed where the leaf joins the stem. It is not necessary to deadhead azaleas, and unlike rhododendrons, they have growth buds all along their stem so you will get new growth close to any cut you make.

Recorded rhododendron history begins in 400 B.C. when tales were told of its leaves being used medicinally. The English in the eighteenth and nineteenth century enthusiastically brought them back from Asia, but the real European rhododendron explosion started in 1830 when Sir Joseph Hooker found forty-five heretofore unknown species in Sikkim. In 1900 there were 300 known rhododendron species and hybrid varieties. Today there are thousands. In the 1920s Lord Lionel Rothchild, a member of the banking clan, spared no money in developing rhododendrons on his estate in Exbury, England. He employed 225 men in his gardens and crossed tens of thousands of plants. The Exbury hybrids are among the finest today.

In the United States some species of rhododendron grow wild (*R. carolinianum, R. maximum*), and it is a beautiful sight to see a hillside in North Carolina covered in the spring with blooming rhododendron. Azaleas, too, grow wild, and the wild ones are all deciduous (*R. arborescens, R. calendulaceum*).

The following list includes some of the best rhododendrons chosen by the American Rhododendron Society. Blooming dates refer to Oregon only; adjust for your own area.

Pink   'Mrs. Furnival'
        Hardy to -10° F.
        Blooms late May
        Pink flowers with light-brown splotches on upper petals

Purple 'Blue Ensign'
        Hardy to -10° F.
        Blooms late May
        Lavender-blue with black spot

Red   'Ruby Bowman'
        Hardy to 0° F.
        Blooms early May
        Wavy 4½-inch flowers which are rose-red with red
            throat

White   'Loder's white'
        Hardy to 0° F.
        Blooms late April
        Pink buds open to frilled, white flowers

Yellow 'Moonstone'
        Hardy to -5° F.
        Blooms mid-April
        Bell-shaped, creamy-yellow flowers which open pink

Many famous hybridizers have worked for over a hundred years to produce evergreen azaleas with spectacular flowers, and each has produced a group of plants with certain characteristics.

Gable hybrids are evergreen azaleas that will withstand zero temperatures. It blooms heavily in April and May.

Glenn Dale hybrids were developed at the United States Division of Plant Exploration and Introduction station at Glenn Dale, Maryland. This is a group of over 300 hybrids which are evergreen and grow from four to eight feet tall. The coloring is wonderful; some varieties have markings of several colors, others are flecked, striped, or blotched with one color over another.

Kurume hybrids have been popular in Japan for over a hundred years. They were hybridized at Kurume on the Japanese island of Kyushu. They are hardy as far north as Philadelphia or where the temperature does not drop below 5° or 10° F.

Brooks hybrids were developed in California to endure hot, dry summers.

Knap Hill and Exbury hybrids are deciduous azaleas which are hardy to -20° F. Knap Hill is the name of the nursery which belonged to Anthony Waterer, and Exbury is the name of the strain of the Rothschild varieties. Lord Rothschild acquired the Knap Hill Nursery. Exbury colors are vivid and blooms are huge.

Ghent hybrids are the hardiest of all the deciduous azaleas. They can withstand temperatures down to -25° F.

Gumpo hybrids are hardy to 5° F. with very large blooms.

Choice Evergreen Azaleas

Lavender	'Sherwood Orchid'
	Kurume type
	Blooms March–April
	Large, red-violet flower
Pink	'Rosaeflora'
	Gumpo type
	Blooms April–May
	Rose-pink, double flowers
Red	'Glamour'
	Glenn Dale type
	Blooms April–May
	Vivid, orange-red flowers
Variegated	'Geisha'

	Glenn Dale type
	Blooms February–March
	White flowers striped with red
White	'Gumpo'
	Gumpo type
	Blooms May–June
	Large, single white flowers

Choice Deciduous Azaleas

Orange	'Gibraltar'
	Exbury type
	Blooms late May
	Big, deep-orange flowers with ruffled edges
Pink	'Rosella'
	Knap type
	Blooms early June
	Large, pale-pink flowers
Red	'Fireball'
	Exbury type
	Blooms June
	Deep-red flowers
White	'Visco Sepala'
	Exbury type
	Blooms May
	Extremely fragrant white flowers
Yellow	'Goldfinch'
	Knap type
	Blooms late May
	Apricot-yellow flowers shading to pink

For further information, write:

The American Rhododendron Society
2232 N.E. 78th Avenue
Portland, Oregon 97213
Dues: $12.00 per annum

Salal, *Gaultheria shallon*

Salal is a popular ground cover on the Pacific coast, but little known in the east, which is a pity because it is an attractive plant.

Grown in poor soil and in full sunlight it makes an excellent mat of rich green. Grown in the shade in moist, acid soil it becomes a 1½-foot woody shrub so valued as an evergreen that the United States Department of Agriculture selected it as one of the thirty best shrubs for shady areas.

Salal has dark-green, heart-shaped, leathery leaves, and in the summer has white to pink flowers. It is reliably hardy as far north as New York City, although some gardeners in the Boston area have had success with it.

Skimmia, *Skimmia japonica*

Skimmia is a real winner in the shade border. It has an exceptionally neat habit of growth, making a three-to-four-foot, round clump with dense, glossy, evergreen leaves and small, yellowish flowers in the spring followed by bright-red berries in the autumn and winter. You won't get any berries unless you have both male and female planted closely together, so be careful to get both when you select your plants. It is easiest to tell them apart in the spring because the female has smaller flowers. Skimmia is an unusually slow grower and there is little need to allow much room for growth when deciding how closely to space your plants.

The plant is not regarded as hardy north of Philadelphia, but I grew mine with great success in Connecticut. Grow it in rich, porous, acid soil enriched with peat and leaf mold.

Skimmia

Viburnum

The Viburnums are a large plant genus with over 100 species. Some are grown for their lovely white or pink flowers; others for their colorful clusters of yellow, orange, or red fruit (berries) which are not only appealing to the human eye, but attract birds to your garden. All have bright-green, serrated leaves which are evergreen in the south and deciduous in the north. Most do well in the shade but do not bloom as profusely. Read your plant catalogs for descriptions of new and beautiful hybrids, but before you are tantalized into purchasing them by the glowing descriptions, remember my warning about sparse bloom in a heavily shaded garden. However if you have light shade you could not select a lovelier shrub.

The viburnums listed here are native plants which are hardy throughout the United States and do well in more than half-shade.

V. acerifolium (mapleleaf viburnum) is suggested by the United States Department of Agriculture as a plant valued for "its ability to grow in the shade and its pale-pink (leaf) color in the fall." It grows from four to six feet.

V. cassinoidea (witherod) grows from eight to twelve feet high and nearly as wide. In June it has clusters of white flowers about three to four inches wide followed by reddish berries which ultimately turn bluish-black.

V. dentatum (arrowwood viburnum) grows from twelve to sixteen feet tall in an upright but spreading form. In the spring it has charming white flowers three inches wide. In the fall it has

deep-blue fruit, and the leaves turn from pale-purple to red. It prefers very moist soil.

V. lentago (nannyberry) is more like a tree, often growing twenty to thirty feet high. Otherwise it is quite similar to witherod viburnum.

V. prunifolium (black haw) grows from ten to fifteen feet high and about three-fourths as wide. It blooms in May with clusters of white, flat-topped flowers, followed by bluish-black berries nearly one-half inch thick. These berries are sometimes used in preserves.

Yew, *Taxus cuspidata, Taxus baccata, Taxus media*

Yews are the most shade tolerant of all the evergreen, needled shrubs, and are very effective when planted with broad or narrow-leaved shrubs for a contrast in texture. Their dark-green foliage offers a contrast in color, too.

Within the yew genus (*Taxus*) there are many species and varieties offering a wide choice of sizes, shapes, and berries. Some have plum-like berries and others have seeds partly enclosed in a fleshy red coat called an "aril." Children should be warned not to eat these pretty berries. The aril is harmless, but the seed inside is poisonous to both man and livestock. Curiously enough, birds relish the arils and void the seed undigested. Yews grow in a wide variety of soils and tolerate conditions unfavorable for almost all evergreens. They prefer cool, moist sites.

The best of all the yews for a shade garden is the Japanese Yew (*Taxus cuspidata*). Its leaves (needles) are very numerous, about one inch long, and taper to a short dark-green tip. It grows from twenty to forty feet high. *Taxus cuspidata nana* is a dwarf form which grows from four to six feet high and *Taxus cuspidata densa* is a compact form rarely over three feet high.

English yew (*Taxus baccata*) is much more difficult to grow than the Japanese yew. If you live in an area which does not get too much summer heat or drying winds, you may have success with this lovely species. In England, where this plant does so well, it grows to sixty feet anr some plants are reputed to be from 800 to 1000 years old. It even played an important part in English folklore, and before the days of gunpowder its boughs were used for making archers' bows. *T. baccata 'repandens'* is a graceful weeping form of English yew.

To tell the difference between the Japanese and English yew, look at the needles. If they gradually taper to the tip it is an English yew. If they abruptly taper to the tip it is a Japanese yew.

There is a hybrid between the English and Japanese called *Taxus media*. It resembles each of its parents in some ways, and there are several varieties.

T. m. hatfieldii is shrubby and columnar.

T. m. hicksii is an upright, dense shrub which can be sheared, and
 is one of the best for evergreen hedges.

T. m. kelseyi has spreading branches.

Ground hemlock (*Taxus canadensis*) is a low, native evergreen, nearly flat and useful as a ground cover in cool northern
areas. It is very tolerant of shade and is often used as an under-
planting among trees. If planted where it gets too much winter
sun its needles turn an unsightly brownish color. It usually doesn't
grow more than four feet tall. But because it is a fast grower it is
best to prune back the strongest shoots each year or the plant may
become too large for its position.

7

❀❀❀❀❀❀❀❀❀❀

Vines—The Versatile Ones

We grow vines for as many reasons as there are varieties of this vegetation. We use them to cover, to screen, to clothe, to drape, to embellish. We use them on walls, trellises, porches, old tree trunks, in pots, boxes, and tubs, on bare ground and steep banks. We use them to bring fragrance into our garden. And we use them just to look at and admire.

I have chosen several delightful vines which are perfect for a shade garden. The fact that they can be useful as well as beautiful is more than enough reason to consider them for your garden. Generally vines are not fussy about soil, and a flowering vine will reward the gardener who prepares its foot-deep bed with topsoil and manure. But a word of caution—most of the vines which do well in the shade, do so well that they can become a pest and take over everything around them.

Bittersweet, *Celastrus scandens, Celastrus losneri*

Bittersweet is one of the most decorative and attractive vines for a shade garden with its gleaming, green leaves in the summer and its orange berries that split open to show scarlet seeds in the fall. You've probably seen dried bunches of these berry-covered, twisted, gnarled stems sold by florists—or even the supermarket—around Thanksgiving time, and at quite fancy prices too.

C. scandens is an unpredictable plant and sometimes, even

after being well established, doesn't have any berries. This is usually, but not always, caused because only one vine has been planted (a female vine), and unless you have one of each sex you will have flowers but no berries. You can't tell the sex of the plant until you see its little greenish-white blooms in the spring. Look into the center of the flower and if you se a swollen-looking pistil in the center, and immature stamens at the side, it's a female. Male flowers have fully developed stamens with powdery pollen. To further complicate matters, some plants have both male and female flowers on the vines.

Chinese bittersweet (*C. losneri*) produces more berries in the shade and some nurseries claim that you do not need to have two plants to be as sure of berries as you do with *C. scandens*. I have found that it is safer to plant both. If the plant is happy in your garden it will run rampant, climbing and coiling around and into everything in its way—so be careful where you plant it. It is hardy throughout the United States.

Boston Ivy, *Parthenocissus tricuspidata*

Although known as Boston ivy, this plant is from Japan. It is one of the strongest and fastest-growing cultivated vines, and can actually cover the entire side of a substantial building in a few years. It has glossy, three-lobed leaves of varying sizes which make a very thick covering especially on brick walls where its rootlets can cling to the slightly rough surface. Because its petioles are long, they can bear the weight of their own leaves and don't need extra

support like its near relative, the Virginia creeper. Its leaves put on a brilliant display of orange and scarlet in the autumn. Prune carefully and constantly before it not only covers your house, but the windows, too. It is hardy throughout the United States.

P. lowi is a miniature Boston ivy and *P. veitchii* is a small-leaved variety with leaves which are purple when young.

Climbing Hydrangea, *Hydrangea petiolaris*

Climbing hydrangea is a truly beautiful deciduous vine with rich-green foliage and eight-inch clusters of showy, white, hydrangea-like flowers in the summer. It climbs by aerial root, and while

it clings tenaciously to stone or brick walls, it does not strangle tree trunks. In time it can grow fifty or sixty feet high, but should be pruned regularly so that it remains a pleasing shape rather than an overpowering mass. It is hardy throughout the United States.

Dutchman's-pipe, *Aristolochia durior*

Dutchman's-pipe is a very old-fashioned vine with heart-shaped leaves that overlap each other. Its small purple and white flowers are most amusing because they resemble a "dutchman's pipe." The vine grows twenty or thirty feet tall in fertile soil, is very hardy, and while it makes a wonderfully dense wall of green, it can be grown at the base of a pergola or arch for its decorative effect. Prune it rather severely to obtain a bushier plant.

Dutchman's-pipe

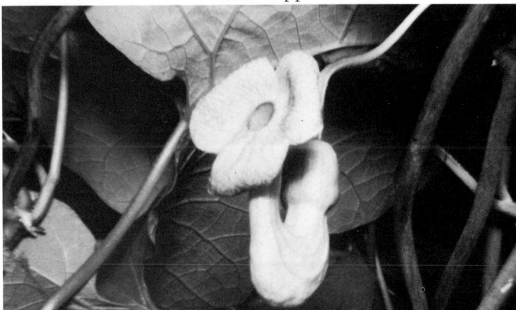

Euonymous (see Chapter 5, page 107)

Five-leaf Akebia (see Chapter 5, page 116)

Honysuckle, *Lonicera japonica halliana,*
Lonicera sempervirens, Lonicera henryi

Honeysuckle takes over everything unless it is tamed. But its tenacity makes it extremely useful in rough, wild areas such as a steep slope or rocky, unattractive ground where there is little nourishment to grow anything. Hall's honeysuckle (*L. japonica halliana*) is excellent wherever you need a quick, thick cover—as long as you keep it under control. It can grow as much as fifteen feet in one year. It has fragrant, white summer flowers and dense green foliage which turns bronze in the fall. It is deciduous and is hardy to Boston.

L. sempervirens (trumpet honeysuckle) has orange-salmon flowers. It does not grow as fast or as rampantly as Hall's honeysuckle. It is deciduous and hardy to Connecticut.

L. henryi has yellow-red flowers and the foliage is evergreen. It is hardy to Maine.

Ivy, (see Chapter 5, page 108)

Moonseed

Moonseed, *Menispermum canadense*

If you have a wet or boggy area where you want a vine, try moonseed. It is attractive, with ivy-shaped leaves and small white flowers which are followed by little seeds shaped like a quarter moon—hence its name. But be warned; it is such a tenacious grower that once started it is almost impossible to get rid of. Even the smallest piece of stem or root will start a new plant. It completely disappears in the winter leaving the ground bare, but returns in the spring with its dense mass of leaves. It is hardy to Boston.

Porcelain Vine, *Ampelopsis brevipedunculata*

Porcelain vine is a strong grower that will literally clothe low walls and flow over rocky areas with the grace of a ballet dancer. It has a three-lobed leaf which belongs to the grape family, but there the resemblance ends. In the autumn its pea-shaped berries look like porcelain, with colors that range from pale-green to lavender and purple, or various shades of aquamarine, turquoise, and ultramarine. Sometimes all the colors appear on one vine simultaneously in one cluster of berries.

Porcelain vine prefers a good garden soil, but will do well on a dry rocky bank. It loses its leaves in the winter except in the extreme southern region of the United States.

Porcelain Vine

Sweet Potato, *Impomoea batatus*

Many people grow sweet potatoes on their kitchen window still so that it will vine around the window. Try it sometime in an outdoor hanging basket, tub, or container. It is delightful with its large leaves and lilac flowers. You can buy your tubers (sweet potatoes) at the grocery store if they haven't been treated with a preservative to keep them plump; otherwise purchase them from a nursery.

Plant sweet potatoes in a light, porous soil and don't bury the tuber too deeply. Keep the soil a little dry so it won't rot until growth is several inches high, then keep fairly moist. At the end of the growing season in the autumn, dig up your beautiful vine and you'll find that you have a dividend—more sweet potatoes.

Virginia Creeper, *Parthenocissus quinquefolia*

Virginia creeper is a very hardy and popular vine, having been used with great success since colonial times, and for good reason. It is an excellent cover for wall, fence, porch, or the side of a building. In the woods it is sometimes confused with poison ivy as the leaf shape is similar. Virginia creeper has five-petaled leaves on a stem; poison ivy has only three. Remember the little rhyme "leaves of three, leave them be."

It is a truly beautiful vine during its entire growing period— a rich dark-green in the summer, and brilliant scarlet and crimson in the fall. Although the stems are bare in the winter, they are not unattractive. It can clamber over stones, walls, and fences, clinging by rootlets with disk-like suction cups. On a high wall it may need the extra support of a light wire because of its many lush leaves. It is hardy throughout the United States.

8

⦿⦿⦿⦿⦿⦿⦿⦿⦿⦿⦿

Bulbs–A Blooming Bonanza

Nothing shakes off winter doldrums with the bright promise of spring as much as the sight of a blue crocus or a buttercup-yellow aconite sticking a cheerful head out of the bleak, bare, wintry ground. There's something pixie-like about these tiny harbingers of spring. The first one to appear—the brave one—cautiously sticks its head out of the ground, takes a look around and if it likes what it sees, passes the word and suddenly, almost without any fanfare, the ground is alive with color.

But crocuses and aconites are only the beginning of an ever-changing parade we can get from bulbs. There's not only a riot of color but a variety of form that make all the bulbs so very satisfying, especially since most require so little care. Most bulbs do well in widely varying conditions of soil and climate and once established, multiply. Thus, every spring your bulb garden becomes bigger and more colorful.

To flower, most bulbs need some sun, but the most beautiful of all grow in the early spring when deciduous trees are still without leaves and plenty of sunlight shines through the bare branches. Such early delights as snowdrops, crocus, anemone, scilla, daffodils, tulips and hyacinths do well under a deciduous tree. I have selected sixteen bulbs in the following pages for your shade garden —summer as well as spring bulbs.

There's really only one important "don't" when you plant bulbs in a shade garden: *Don't* plant them under any shallow, rooted trees such as maples, horse chestnuts, or beech. They can't stand the competition of the trees' roots. If you want color under those trees, plant your bulbs in tubs or containers. Remember too, that a conifer or broad-leaved evergreen screens out sunlight. Plant your bulbs in front of them, not under them. Most tender bulbs, especially tuberous begonias, can be damaged by wind. If you can place them in a protected location, all the better. If not, improvise something for use as a windbreak.

It is vital for bulbs to have good drainage—something shady soil does not usually have. A quick, easy way to change that is to put a little sand in the hole you dig for each bulb—not seashore sand, but builder's or construction sand.

The great variety of bulbs we are blessed with are classified many different ways—bulbs, tubers, corms, or pips—but don't be confused, it's only a technicality. The most important thing you must know about bulbs is whether they are hardy (planted in the fall) or tender (planted in the late spring).

Hardy bulbs must be put into the ground in the fall because they need the cold weather to make them bloom. These include most of the bulbs which bloom in the spring such as the tulip, the daffodil, and the crocus. Tender bulbs, often referred to as spring bulbs (though they don't bloom in the spring), must be planted in the spring after the soil has warmed up (about tomato planting time, or just after Memorial Day). If you want to keep them for the following year, they must be dug up in the fall and stored in a frost-free area during the winter. Tender bulbs are best started indoors about six to eight weeks before going into the garden. These include caladiums with their fabulous foliage in red and green, green and white, pink and green, green with pink spots, and literally endless combinations of these four colors—a must for every shade garden. Another "must" in the tender bulb category is elephant ear's with huge leaves from two to four feet in width which grow on stalks as tall as the leaves are wide. Another summer-blooming gem is achimenes with lovely arching stems covered with crimson, violet, or white flowers resembling long-necked velvety pansies.

SPRING BULBS

Achimenes, *Achimenes*

Achimenes is an attractive, summer-blooming plant which grows from twelve to twenty-four inches tall and has arching stems covered with little crimson, violet, or white blooms which resemble long-necked, velvety pansies. They are usually grown for window boxes or hanging baskets, but they are excellent for use as a bedding or edging plant in a shady garden when set about ten inches apart.

They develop from tubers which should be started indoors between February and April. Plant the tubers one inch deep in a mixture of equal parts of peat moss, sand, leaf mold, and soil which is kept damp but not wet. Set it out in the garden when all danger of cold weather is past. Pinch back to keep it full and bushy, and add a dilute liquid fertilizer every other week during the growing season. You will have blooms all summer long, and in autumn bring the plants back into the house, let them dry out, and then store the clumps in a paper bag until you are ready to start them again the following year. They can be grown from seed as well as tubers, but the process takes two years.

Some varieties include:

A. *coccinea*—crimson
A. *chiesbreghtii*—crimson-scarlet
A. *tubiflora*—white

Caladium

Caladiums are superb in a shady garden. They are grown for their colorful leaves, not their flowers. But what spectacular leaves they have! Large, heart-shaped beauties from six to ten inches long and five to eight inches wide with a tropical look about them. These elegant leaves are variegated in a wide variety of handsome, multi-colored patterns—red and green, green and white, pink and green, green with pink spots, green and red with lilac spots, white with red blotches, and pink and white with green ribs. All have prominent, strongly colored veins which heighten the dramatic effect.

They are grown from a tuber which may be planted outdoors

in the south as soon as the weather is warm. In the north they should be started indoors eight weeks before putting them outside. Don't be in a rush to put them outdoors if you live in an area prone to a late cold spell.

To start them indoors, put each tuber into a five-inch pot in a mixture of equal parts of good garden soil, peat moss, leaf mold, manure, and sand, and cover their tops with about two inches of the mixture. Keep barely damp until they become active—barely damp, not wet—and don't kill them with kindness or they will rot. Keep in a warm (seventy to eighty degrees) humid place. When you see leaves beginning to sprout, water freely and use a mild liquid fertilizer twice each month. Mild, half the strength the directions call for. Harden them before planting outdoors by moving them to gradually cooler locations.

I plant mine outdoors right in the pot in which it was grown, but you may prefer to remove the tuber from the pot and plant it directly in the ground. It doesn't matter which way you do it as long as they have well-drained, moist soil and are placed in a shady area protected from the wind. The plants grow from twelve to twenty-four inches tall. In the early fall, before frost sets in, remove the pot from the ground and stop watering. Let the plant die naturally with the foliage intact. When all the foliage is dead, cut it off and store pot and tuber in a moderately warm place.

Varieties:

C. 'Ace of Hearts', red and green
C. 'Candidum', white with green veins
C. 'Edith Mead', white with green edges and red veins
C. 'John Peed', metallic red and moss green
C. 'Keystone' green with pink veins and spots
C. 'Macahyba', green and red with lilac spots
C. 'Marie Moir', white with red blotches
C. 'Sorocaba', pink and white with green ribs

Elephant's Ear, *Colocasia antiquorum*

Colocasia gets its common name from beautiful, green, elephant-ear-shaped leaves. The huge leaves grow on stalks from two to four feet tall and spread out almost as wide. Allow plenty of room between plants when you set them outside. The tubers can

be planted directly in the garden in the southern part of the United States, but in northern regions they should be grown like caladiums (p. 177). They should be fertilized weekly. Be sure they don't dry out in the summer garden; they must be kept moist.

C. *esculenta* is "taro root," which is edible and often sold in Latin-American vegetable markets.

Tuberous Begonias

On any list of the most beautiful flowers in the world, tuberous begonias ought to be near the top. Some would put them at the head of such a list. Some are frilled, ruffled, or crested; others look like a waxy camellia or the flowers of a carnation. Some are single, some double. Some are compact and erect, others are pendulous. Some have flowers which are four to six inches wide. All come in a variety of colors that never fails to astonish me—pure white, cream, shocking pink, scarlet, salmon, orange, yellow, and apricot. Some are only one color; others are variegated, streaked, or edged with a second color. All are fabulous!

All also require shade. Why, then, don't we see them growing in every shady garden? It's because they like a cool, damp climate where summer nights are not hot. In the Pacific Northwest you can see sensational specimens. Try to grow the same variety in New York City and you may be disappointed.

They grow from tubers which can be planted outdoors after all danger of frost is past, but it is usually best to start them indoors if you want them to bloom early in the summer. Plant with the hollow side up, in a mixture of leaf mold and sand. When growing only a few, cut half-gallon milk cartons lengthwise to get shallow containers. Place the tubers on top of the sand mix; don't cover it. Keep them moist, but not wet. This is particularly important since they will rot if kept too wet. When your container is filled with roots it is time to plant each tuber separately in four-or-five-inch pots. Carefully lift the tuber and roots and plant them in a rich soil mixed with plenty of sand or perlite for good drainage, then cover them with one or two inches of the soil mix. Sink the pot up to the rim in the garden as soon as the weather is warm enough. Fertilize with a diluted liquid fertilizer every week. Remind yourself to do it on the first and fifteenth of the month. Most tuberous begonias need to be staked and tied to keep the weight of the blooms from breaking the stems of the plant.

HARDY BULBS

Aconite, *Eranthis*

Even before the crocus blooms in the spring, aconite peeps its little head out of the ground, even in the worst weather conditions. Aconites have dainty, little, yellow flowers which look a little like buttercups, and grow about three inches high. They do well under

trees where few other plants can hold their own. They seed themselves freely and colonies are soon formed from self-sown seed. They like rich, loose, woodsy, moist soil. Don't wait until autumn to plant the tubers. Plant in July or August.

Squills, *Scilla hispanica, Scilla sibirica, Scilla nonscripta*

Blooming in the spring, squills with their dainty, bell-shaped flowers are a marvelous addition to woodland or rock garden, and also are excellent for use as a border or edging plant. Never plant them singly, but use at least twelve to eighteen bulbs in a group.

Plant them in the fall about four to five inches deep and three inches apart in rich, moist, woodsy soil. Once established they last a lifetime, multiply freely, and require no care.

S. *hispanica*, sometimes called wood hyacinths, grows about twelve to fifteen inches tall. There are white, blue, or pink varieties.

S. *sibirica* grows only a few inches high, and has a more open, bell-shaped flower than S. *hispanica*. There are white and blue varieties.

S. *nonscripta*, sometimes called English bluebell, grows from twelve to eighteen inches tall. There are varieties with blue, white, or pink flowers which are fragrant.

Camassia

Camassia is a flower you don't see in too many spring gardens. It is a pity because it is hardy and thrives under ordinary conditions or when naturalized in moist woods. Its flower stems are from two to four feet high, and have as many as a hundred purple, star-shaped flowers 1½ inches wide which bloom in long succession. Plant it in early fall, four to five inches deep and six to nine inches apart.

C. *esculenta* is excellent for wet areas where other bulbs will not survive.

C. *cusickii* resembles C. *esculenta* but is larger, and its flowers are a deep blue.

Camassia

Crocus

The Dutch crocus is such a familiar spring flower that many people do not know there is more than one species. Some bloom much earlier in the spring, others in the autumn. Like the Dutch crocus, these species and hybrids have gay little purple, blue, white, or yellow flowers on five-inch stems. But unlike the Dutch crocus which has a globular shape, their blooms open wide to an almost star-like form. Both the Dutch crocus and other species and hybrids are planted in the fall. All are very hardy, and once planted appear each year and multiply by leaps and bounds from year to year. They are truly work-free plants.

Dutch Crocus
C. 'Enchantress'—porcelain-blue
C. 'Snow Storm'—pure-white
C. 'Striped Beauty'—lilac-striped white
C. 'Yellow Mammoth'—golden-yellow
Autumn Flowering Crocus
C. 'Medius'—violet
C. 'Speciosus Albus'—white
C. 'Zonatus'—rose-lilac
Crocus Species and Hybrids (Very early spring bloomers)
C. 'Snow Bunting'—white flowers with golden throat
C. 'Canary Bird'—yellow, bronze outside
C. 'Ruby Giant'—deep-violet
C. 'Chrysanthus Blue Giant'—bright-blue

Crocus can be potted in October for indoor bloom at Christmas by placing bulbs in moist pebbles or peat (the same process used for paper-white narcissus).

Cyclamen, *Cyclamen*

The hardy cyclamen is very much like the familiar greenhouse variety. It is a little plant, growing only four inches high, with literally hundreds of small, delicately sweet-scented flowers which bloom in late summer or early autumn. When they are finished blooming they lose their leaves and completely disappear. Mark the

spot so that you do not damage the corms when you cannot see them. It should be planted in July, about 1 to 1½ inches deep in good garden soil which is porous and constantly moist.

C. europaeum is red and blooms in late summer and fall.
C. neapolitanum is rose or cream-colored and blooms in September.

Daffodils, *Narcissus*

Daffodils grow in the shade even though they are not shade-loving plants. Why? George S. Lee, Jr., expert horticulturist from Connecticut, explained it very well in an article he wrote for the Brooklyn Botanic Garden in their pamphlet on "Gardening in the Shade."

> . . . The brief part of their life cycle which is spent above ground draws to a close as the new growth appears on trees and shrubs. By the time the leaves of woody plants unfold, the embryonic flowers have been formed for another year, the scales of the bulbs are packed with starch in anticipation of dormancy. . . . They must flower and mature in sunlight screened by nothing more opaque than the bare framework of deciduous shrubs and trees.

Don't ever grow them under broad-leaved or coniferous evergreens. If you grow them under trees, even deeply rooted ones, don't forget to give them extra food. Check the fertilizer label. Choose one with a high content of potash.

Certain daffodils grow better than others in the shade. For example, the most popular of all daffodils, the 'King Alfred' does not flower well except in full sun. I have selected only those varieties which will do well in the shade. All are early varieties which bloom while the leaves of most deciduous trees are still bare.

N. 'Artic Gold'—yellow
N. 'Ardelinis'—white
N. 'Spellbinder'—yellow and white
N. 'Ardour'—yellow and orange
N. 'Ludlow'—white
N. 'Ceylon'—yellow and red
N. 'Content'—white and yellow

A miniature daffodil measuring, as the ruler indicates, only six inches.

Glory-of-the-snow, *Chionodaxa*

Glory-of-the-snow is a dainty little spring bulb which is hardy, trouble-free, and looks beautiful massed in a rock garden, border woodland, or naturalized garden. It multiplies naturally and easily. They grow from three to six inches tall and have many star-shaped,

sky-blue flowers on a stem. Plant them in the early fall two inches deep and two to three inches apart.

C. Luciliae is bright-blue with a white center.
C. lucillae alba is pure white.
C. lucillae rosea is pink.

Grape Hyacinth, *Muscari*

Grape hyacinths have been well-named. Their eight-inch stems have clusters of flowers tightly squeezed together like a bunch of tiny grapes. Their foliage is grass-like and often reappears in the fall. They self-sow easily and are effective in little colonies in a rock garden. Plant them in early fall, two inches deep and two to three inches apart. Don't use fewer than twelve to eighteen bulbs per square foot.

M. armeniacum is a deep cobalt-blue.
M. botryoides albus is white.
M. plumosum is violet.

Grape Hyacinth

Hyacinth, *Hyacinthus*

Hyacinths are proud, erect flowers which stand from twelve to eighteen inches tall on strong stems, and have cylindrical flower

spikes densely covered with bell-shaped blooms of blue, white, yellow, pink, or red. They have a heady, heavy perfume. Once planted they may be left in place, but blooms tend to become smaller and sparser unless the bulbs are lifted after the foliage has died down. Store them in a dry cool place and replant in the fall.

Some choice varieties are:

H. 'Princess Margaret'—light-pink
H. 'City of Haarlem'—yellow
H. 'Jan Bos'—carmine-red
H. 'L'innocence'—pure-white
H. 'Orange Boven'—orange-salmon

Indoors, hyacinths can be grown in water. In October or November, place in a vase made especially for hyacinths, which is tall, tapered, and cup-shaped at the top to prevent the bulb from having more than its base submerged in the water. Put the glass and bulb in a cool, dark closet where the temperature stays between 40° F. and 50° F. When there is four inches of growth, place the glass and bulb in a moderately warm room (70° F.) which has strong light, but avoid sunlight.

Snowdrops, *Galanthus*

Snowdrops are one of the very early spring bulbs and are often in bloom while there is still frost on the ground. They look best planted in colonies where they can form masses of snow-white flowers. They require very little attention and can remain undisturbed for years and years. In August or September, plant them two to

four inches apart and two to three inches deep in rich, moist woodland soil.

Snowflake, *Leucojum*

Snowflake is a charming spring bulb with an abundance of little, green-tipped, white, bell-like flowers on twelve inch stems.
They resemble snowdrops in their habit of growth, but I prefer
snowflakes not only because I find them prettier, but because you
don't see them so frequently. They are particularly attractive for

floral arrangements and last well when cut. Plant them two inches deep and one to two inches apart in porous, moist soil. Once planted, don't disturb them.

Star-of-bethlehem, *Ornithogalum*

Star-of-bethlehem is a charming plant for a woodland or naturalized garden, and grows six to ten inches tall. In the spring it has pure-white, star-like flowers which last well when used in floral arrangements. It spreads freely and is a delight. It likes rich soil which is porous. Prepare the soil well with manure and compost or leaf mold and plant bulbs one to two inches below the surface.

Other hardy species include:

O. narbonense which is eighteen inches tall and blooms in early summer.

O. nutans which is twelve to eighteen inches tall and blooms in spring.

O. pyramidale which is twenty-four inches tall and blooms in summer.

O. umbellatum which is six to ten inches tall and blooms in spring.

There are also tender varieties, but most of these require more sun than shade.

Striped Squill, *Puschkinia scilloides*

Striped squill is a tiny rock garden plant with beautiful, little white flowers striped with a soft, clear blue. It grows only five or six inches tall. Don't plant single bulbs—plant in a cluster for a greater effect. Plant them two to three inches deep in the fall in rich, moist, woodland soil.

Striped Squill

Trout Lilies, *Erythronium*

There are wild trout lilies which grow in the woods, and there are cultivated hybrids. If you find the wild ones in the woods, leave them there and don't try to bring them into your home garden. They don't transplant easily and the hybrids are superior anyway.

Trout lilies grow on six-to-ten-inch stems and have little, lily-like flowers in delicate colors and tints of white, pink, cream, bright-yellow, and rose. They love to be in wooded places under shrubs or in shady corners or crevices of a rock garden. Plant them in late August or early September, three inches deep and two to three inches apart. They like to be kept moist in rich, woodland soil full of humus. Once planted, leave them alone. They don't like to be moved.

Trout lilies

Tulip, *Tulipa*

Tulips are too well-known to need description. Pick up any bulb catalog and you will find page after page of pictures of perfect tulips to tantalize you. Some are fringed, and others are shaped like a lily or peony. Some grow almost three feet tall, others only a few inches.

Tulips are generally categorized into the following groups.

Botanical types which have three main species: *kaufmanniana, fosteriana,* and *greigii,* which bloom in that order. They are usually only a few inches tall.

Cottage tulips are oval in shape with recurved petals. They are usually from twenty-six to twenty-eight inches tall and are very graceful.

Darwin tulips have strong, sturdy stems and usually grow thirty inches tall. They bloom later than cottage tulips.

Fringed tulips have long-lasting flowers with fringed petals and grow twenty-six to twenty-eight inches tall. They are spectacular.

Peony-flowered tulips have enormous, peony-shaped flowers and grow from sixteen to twenty inches tall.

Parrot tulips are great for floral arrangements, but are not effective when used in borders or beds because their stem is often not strong enough to support the weight of the flower. They are unusual and you may be fascinated by their huge blossoms with irregularly shaped, two-tone petals.

Bouquet tulips produce three, four, or more tulips from a single bulb. They grow twenty to twenty-eight inches tall.

If you want your tulips to look like the pictures in the catalogs there are a few things you must remember. Buy large size bulbs and you'll get bigger, better flowers. The best bulbs are only a little more expensive than the ordinary ones. Plant as late as possible in the fall. Should your bulbs arrive early in the season, keep them where the temperature does not rise above seventy degrees or the flowers produced will not be as large. Plant them five to eight inches deep. If you are troubled by mice or squirrels, plant them ten to twelve inches deep. Most rodents won't dig down that far. Plant in well-drained soil. Tulips, and most other bulbs for that matter do not like wet feet. Plant in an area where the shade comes from trees whose new leaves don't arrive until late in the spring. If there is any doubt about this, choose tulip varieties which bloom early in the season.

The following varieties have been chosen for no other reason than that they are my favorites.

T. 'Burbundy Lace' I first saw this twenty-eight-inch-tall, rich, wine-colored, fringed tulip at the Keukenhof Gardens at Lisse, and was so·enchanted by it that I ordered my bulbs before I left Holland. One catalog describes the fringed petals as having " . . . an effect almost as though a layer of very fragile ice crystals had formed along the rim of the flaring, goblet-like flowers."

T. 'Clara Carder' is an eighteen-inch beauty with a white center and pink petals, and has enormous flowers resembling peonies. It is an Award of Merit winner.

T. 'White Triumphator' is an eighteen-inch-tall, lily-flowered tulip with pure-white, pointed petals. It is extremely graceful.

T. 'Orange Emperor' is a flamboyant, apricot-colored tulip of the fosteriana type which grows fourteen inches tall and has elegance and style. I have seen an interesting all-orange garden with oranges, roses, orange impatiens, and orange tulips. It was most effective.

T. 'Gaiety' is a tulip of the Kaufmaniannina type. It grows only four inches high and is pure-white inside. The outside is striped red.

T. 'Rose Mist' is a bouquet-type tulip. Each stem has four or more flowers which are white with rose-colored edges.

APPENDIX 1

✿✿✿✿✿✿✿✿✿✿✿

Regional Selection of Shade-loving Plants

In this book I have included shade-loving plants for every area of the United States. Since climatic conditions vary greatly across the nation this book would not be complete without a chapter on regional advice. It has been compiled from a cross section of information furnished by thirty-one of the most competent and knowledgeable botanists and horticulturists working with Botanical Gardens, Arboreta, Public Gardens and Horticultural Societies across the United States.

I asked which shrubs, ground covers, annuals, and perennials did well in their region in FULL SHADE. I did not equivocate with the definition of "full shade" because I wanted to make it abundantly clear that I was not asking for their experiences in growing in half-shade or part sun. I also asked for helpful hints for the amateur gardener faced with the problem of gardening in the shade. The complete list of those who cooperated in compiling this chapter can be found at the end of this section. Their responses were extraordinarily interesting and revealing.

To tabulate the lists I divided the United States into six regions:

New England states
Eastern states (from New York City to Maryland)
Central states
Southern states
California (San Francisco and south)
Pacific Northwestern states

The lists were interesting as much for their dissimilarity as for their general agreement. In the east, for example, the most popular shrubs by far were Skimmia, leucothoë and andromeda. In the central states, only witch hazel (*Hamamelis virginiana*) was listed by more than two Botanical Gardens.

Among the ground covers there was more unanimity. Myrtle (*vinca*), bugle (*ajuga*), Japanese spurge (*pachysandra*), ivy (*Hedera*) and *euonymus* were popular in the east. Myrtle and ivy were selected in New England and the central states. Ivy was the only ground cover selected by *every* region.

All the botanical gardens agreed that annuals were the most difficult to grow in the shade. C. Roy Boutard, who has been the Horticultural Director of the Berkshire Garden Center in Stockbridge, Massachusetts for over twenty years wrote,

"Annuals—forget it! I can't think of a single one . . . for FULL shade. Impatiens and coleus will grow in shade, but not full shade."

Refer back to Chapter 1 where I defined plants which would grow in the shade as those needing strong light all day plus two or three hours of sunshine. It took a lot of research and thought to select plants for this kind of shade. Most garden books, when dealing with shade, include those plants that will grow under sunny conditions with some "light, filtered or even half-shade." It is my belief that any conscientious gardener can grow all but a few plants in half-sun. After all, isn't that the same as half-shade? But I well understand Roy Boutard's comment about annuals in "full shade"—for that means strong light, but no sun. I deliberately made the task more difficult for the horticulturists working at the various botanical gardens because I felt it would be more interesting for my readers if they had a plant selection chosen for *full shade.*

Lee Schwade, the Botanist-Horticulturist of the Denver Botanic Gardens in Colorado wrote, "Our shade conditions are peculiar in that the light intensity is so great at this altitude that it is possible to grow plants that would not grow in similar shade conditions of lower altitudes, of course, soil and other factors being equal."

Perennials are a wide category because they take in wildflowers, ferns, and hardy bulbs, as well as cultivated, flowering plants. So the selection was wide not only because of region, but because there are so many plants to choose from. May apple (*Podophyllum peltatum*) was the overwhelming favorite. In the central states, Hosta and Christmas fern (*Polystichum acrostichoides*) headed the lists. In the south and California, no single plant emerged as an overwhelming favorite. In the six regional areas the following are the plants selected by the majority of Botanical Gardens. There is no single plant that appeared on every list.

	Regions (of a possible 5) making selection
Shrubs	
Acuba japonica	3
Andromeda	3
Euonymous fortunei	4
Hamamelis virginiana	3
Ilex	3
Kalmia	3
Leucothoë	3
Mahonia	4
Rhododendron	3
Ground Covers	
Ajuga	4
Convallaria majallis	3
Hedera	5
Pachysandra	4
Vinca	4
Annuals	
Begonia semperflorens	4
Impatiens	5
Myosotis (biennial)	5
Perennials	
Adiantum	4
Astilbe	5
Cimicifuga racemosa	3
Dicentra	4
Hosta	4
Viola	4

Many of the botanical gardens stressed the need to pay close attention to the cause of the shade and the amount of water the plants receive. Edward Lindemann of the Pennsylvania State university Botanic Garden summed it up when he wrote, "Quite often the shade itself is not as critical as the source of the shade. Competition for moisture and nutrients under large trees and shrubs causes more harm than the actual shade."

Robert G. Titus of Planting Fields Arboretum in New York warned,

> Plants listed will grow in shade, but may not be able to compete with tree roots of maple, beech, etc. Gardens in the shade may require periodic replacement of plants. Mulching and adequate watering are essential to success.

Henri Schaepman of the National Academy of Science in Washington, D.C. asked all gardeners to ". . . make sure all other growth factors are optimum. Do not compound the disadvantage of shady locations with poor soil conditions, poor drainage, poor ventilation, etc."

Robert J. Dingwall, Chief Horticulturist of the Missouri Botanical Garden in St. Louis, reminded us to ". . . prepare ground well and add plenty of organic matter. Water in dry periods."

Gary Koller, the curator of the Morris Arboretum in Philadelphia, shared my view of shade when he wrote, ". . . view the situation as an asset rather than a liability."

Charles D. Webster, President of the Horticultural Society of New York, joined with Larry G. Pardue, its Executive Director, and said, ". . . ask what I can do to lessen the amount of shade? A reflective fence or surface may be of help. On occasion just one branch clipped properly makes all the difference. Proper pruning may make it possible for the shade gardener to have his cake (herbs etc) and shade too."

Wayne L. Hansis from the UCLA Botanical Garden took a practical view and suggested gardeners should, ". . . cut back, thin out, remove and in other ways get rid of the plants causing extreme shade. Live with the structure causing shade conditions and use shade-loving plants, sacrificing flowers in many cases."

Merle M. Moore from the Matthaei Botanical Gardens in Ann Arbor added two practical pointers, ". . . water early in the day to allow foliage to dry before evening. Avoid overfertilization with nitrogen because the resulting soft growth is highly susceptible to disease attack." And the Berkshire Garden Center's Roy Boutard (bless him!) said people should ". . . read your book. I try to tell people this or that will *not* grow in the shade, but they still plant them there."

The complete list of those who helped compile this information follows:

Arboretum of the Barnes Foundation, Merion, Pennsylvania. List prepared by Dr. John M. Fogg Jr., Director.

Balboa Park Botanical Gardens, Balboa, California. List prepared by Robert V. Murphy, Nursery Supervisor.

Berkshire Garden Center, Stockbridge, Massachusetts. List prepared by C. Roy Boutard, Horticultural Director.

Botanic Garden of the Chicago Horticultural Society. List prepared by James F. Fauss, Horticulturist.

Botanic Garden of Smith College, Northampton, Massachusetts. List prepared by Guy Armstrong, Director.

Brookgreen Gardens, A Society for Southeastern Fora and Fauna, Murrells Inlet, South Carolina. List prepared by Gurdon L. Tarbox Jr., Director.

Campus Arboretum of Haverford College, Haverford, Pennsylvania. List prepared by Ann Bagley, Executive Secretary, Horticulturist.

Denver Botanic Gardens, Denver, Colorado. List prepared by Lee Schwade, Botanist-Horticulturist.

Duke University Sarah P. Duke Gardens, Durham, North Carolina. List prepared by Larry T. Daniel, Assistant Director.

Finch Arboretum, Spokane, Washington. List prepared by Thomas J. Banko, Arboriculturist.

Holmdel Arboretum, Freehold, New Jersey. List prepared by David C. Shaw, Superintendent, Monmouth County Shade Tree Commission and Holmdel Arboretum.

Horticultural Society of New York, New York City, New York. List prepared by Charles D. Webster, President.

Longwood Gardens Inc., Kennett Square, Pennsylvania. List prepared by Everitt L. Miller, Assistant Director.

Meadowbrook Farm, Meadowbrook, Pennsylvania. List prepared by Mrs. Norman Fisher.

Matthaei Botanical Gardens, Ann Arbor, Michigan. List prepared by Merle M. Moore, Senior Horticulturist.

Missouri Botanical Garden, St. Louis, Missouri. List prepared by Robert J. Dingwall, Chief Horticulturist.

Morris Arboretum, Philadelphia, Pennsylvania. List prepared by Gary Koller, Curator.

National Academy of Science, Washington, D.C. List prepared by Henri Schaepman, Grounds Supervisor.

New York Botanical Garden, Bronx, New York. List prepared by Karl Grieshaber, Horticultural Specialist.

Pennsylvania Horticultural Society's 18th Century Garden, Philadelphia, Pennsylvania. List prepared by Edward L. Lindemann, Staff Horticulturist.

Pennsylvania State University College of Agriculture, in cooperation with the United States Department of Agriculture. List prepared by J. Robert Nuss, Extension Specialist in Ornamental Horticultures.

Planting Fields Arboretum, Oyster Bay, New York. List prepared by Robert G. Titus, Assistant Director.

R. S. Barnwell Memorial Garden and Art Center, Shreveport, Louisiana. List prepared by J. W. White, Ph.D., area Horticultural Agent.

Santa Barbara Botanical Garden, Santa Barbara, California. List prepared by Mr. Dara E. Emery, Horticulturist.

Strybing Arboretum, San Francisco, California. List prepared by John E. Buyan, Director.

The B–J's Garden Nursery, Eugene, Oregon. List prepared by Charmian Byers-Jones, Owner.

The John A. Finch Arboretum, Spokane, Washington. List prepared by Dr. Tom Banko, Arboriculturist, and Ed Bettinger, Head Gardener.

University of Alberta Botanic Garden, Edmonton, Alberta, Canada. List prepared by Mrs. Gillian Ford, Assistant Curator.

The Morton Arboretum, Lisle, Illinois. List prepared by W. R. Crowley, Head of Plant Information.

University of California at Los Angeles Botanical Garden, Biology Department, Los Angeles, California. List prepared by Wayne L. Hensis, UCLA Botanical Garden Manager.

University of Minnesota Landscape Arboretum, Chaska, Minnesota. List prepared by Mervin C. Eisel.

University of Washington Arboretum, Spokane, Washington. List prepared by Joseph Witt.

Yale University Marsh Gardens, New Haven, Connecticut. List prepared by Mr. Leonard Sablitz, Superintendent.

APPENDIX 2

✤✤✤✤✤✤✤✤✤✤✤

Regional Lists of Shade-loving Plants

Selected by botanical gardens, arboreta, public gardens and horticultural societies

---

SHRUBS

East (New York City and Long Island, south to Maryland)

Botanical name	*Common name*
Abelia grandiflora	Glossy Abelia
Abeliophyllum distichum	Korean Abelia-leaf
Aucuba japonica	Japanese Aucuba
Alnus (species)	Alders
Amelanchier canadensis	Shadblow
Andromeda glaucophylla	Downy Andromeda
A. prolifolia	Bog Rosemary
Aronia (species)	Chokeberry
Berberis thunbergii	Japanese Barberry
Calycanthus floridus	Common Sweetshrub
Camellia japonica	Camellia
C. sasanqua	Sasanqua Camellia
Cercis canadensis	Eastern Redbud
Clethra alnifolia	Summersweet
Daphne odora	Fragrant Daphne
Elaeagnus angustifolius	Russian Olive
Euonymus alatus	Winged Euonymus
Euonymus kiautschovicus	Spreading Euonymus
Forsythia (species)	Forsythias
Fothergilla gardenii	Dwarf Fothergilla

Botanical name	Common name
Gaylussacia baccata	Black Huckleberry
Hamamelis virginiana	Common Witch Hazel
Hydrangea quercifolia	Oakleaf Hydrangea
Ilex aquifolum	Holly
I. cornuta	Chinese Holly
I. crenata	Japanese Holly
I. glabra	Inkberry
I. rugosa	Rugose Holly
Kalmia latifolia	Mountain Laurel
Leucothoë axillaris	Coast Leucothoë
L. catesbaei	Drooping Leucothoë
L. racemosa	Fetterbush
Lindera benzoin	Spicebush
Mahonia aquifolium	Oregon Holly Grape
M. bealii	Leatherleaf Mahonia
M. repens	Dwarf Holly Grape
Myrica Pensylvanica	Northern Bayberry
Oxydendrum arboreum	Sourwood
Rhododendron calendulaceum	Flame Azalea
R. carolinianum	Carolina Rhododendron
R. maximum	Rosebay Rhododendron
R. obtusum	Hiryu Azalea
R. (species)	Rhododendrons & Azaleas
Sarcococca hookeriana	Fragrant Sarcococca
Skimmia japonica	Japanese Skimmia
Stephanandra incisa	Cutleaf Stephanandra
Taxus baccata repandens	Spreading English Yew
Viburnum acerifolium	Mapleleaf Viburnum
V. alnifolium	Hobblebush
Xanthorhiza simplicissima	Yellowroot

New England

Botanical name	Common name
Acanthopanax sieboldianus	Five-leaf Aralia
Akebia quinata	Five-leaf Akebia
Vaccinium (species)	Blueberries
Euonymus fortunei vegetus	Wintercreeper
Ilex crenata	Japanese Holly
Kalmia latifolia	Mountain Laurel
Leucothoë catesbaei	Drooping Leucothoë
Lonicera tartarica	Tatarian Honeysuckle
Pieris floribunda	Mountain Andromeda
Rhododendron (species)	Rhododendrons, Azaleas
Sorbaria sorbifolia	False Spirea

Central (Illinois, Michigan, Minnesota south to Missouri, west to Colorado)

Botanical name	Common name
Acanthopanax sieboldianus	Five-leaf Aralia
Aronia (species)	Chokeberry
Asimina triloba	Pawpaw or Papaw
Buxus microphylla koreana	Korean Littleleaf Boxwood
Clethra alnifolia	Summersweet
Dirca palustris	Leatherwood
Euonymus europaeus	Euonymus
E. fortunei vegetus	Wintercreeper

Botanical name	Common name
E. fortunei radicans	
E. fortunei 'Sarcoxie'	
Hamamelis virginiana	Common Witch Hazel
Hydrangea arborescens	Smooth Hydrangea
H. quericiofolia	Oakleaf Hydrangea
Ilex crenata	Japanese Holly
Ilex (species)	Hollies
Kalmia angustifolia	Sheep Laurel
Leucothoë catesbaei	Drooping Leucothoë
Lindera benzoin	Spicebush
Mahonia aquifolium	Oregon Holly Grape
Myrica Pensylvanica	Bayberry
Nandina domestica	Nandina
Philadelphus coronarius	Sweet Mock Orange
Pieris japonica	Japanese Andromeda
Pyracantha (species)	Firethorn
Rhamnus cathartica	Common Buckthorn
Ribes alpinum	Alpine Currant
Rubus odoratus	Flowering Raspberry
Smilax hispida	Hispid Greenbrier
Sorbaria sorbifolia	False Spirea
Staphylea trifolia	American Bladdernut
Taxus (species)	Yew
Vaccinum	Blueberry
Viburnum acerifolium	Mapleleaf Viburnum
V. burkwoodii	Burkwood Viburnum
V. dentatum	Arrowwood
V. lentago	Nannyberry
V. trilobum	American Cranberry Bush

South (Washington, D.C., South Carolina south to Louisiana)

Botanical name	Common name
Aesculus pavia	Red Buckeye
Ardisia crispa	Christmas Berry
Aucuba japonica	Japanese Aucuba
Buxus sempervirens	Boxwood
Camellia japonica	Camellia
Daphne odora	Fragrant Daphne
Fatsia japonica	Japanese Fatsia
Gardenia radicans	Dwarf Gardenia
Hamamelis virginiana	Common Witch Hazel
Hydrangea macrophylla	House Hydrangea
H. quericiofolia	Oakleaf Hydrangea
Ilex vomitoria nana	Dwarf Yaupon Holly
Kalmia latifolia	Mountain Laurel
Rhododendrons (kurume hybrids)	Azaleas
Mahonia aquifolium	Oregon Holly Grape
Osmanthus fragrans	Sweet Osmanthus
Rhododendron (species)	Azaleas

California (San Francisco south to San Diego)

Botanical name	Common name
Aucuba japonica	Japanese Aucuba
Arctostaphylos edmundsii	Little Sur Manzanita

Botanical name	Common name
A. hookeri	Hooker Manzanita
Aspidistra elatior	Cast Iron Plant
Berberis darwinii	Darwin Barberry
Camellia japonica	Camellia
Chlorophytum elatum	Spider Plant
Clivia miniata	Scarlet Kaffir Lily
Drimys lanciolata	Drimys
Eranthemum nervosum	Winterblue
Euonymus fortunei vegetus	Wintercreeper
Fuchsia (species)	Fuchsia
Gaultheria shallon	Salal, Shallon
Illicium religiosum	Anisetree
Mahonia aquifolium	Oregon Holly Grape
M. lomariifolia	Mahonia
Mysine africana	African Boxwood
Pieris formosa	Himalayan Andromeda
P. japonica	Japanese Andromeda
Pittosporum tobira	Japanese Pittosporum
Rhamnus californica	Coffeeberry
Ribes speciosum	Flowered Gooseberry
R. viburnifolium	Evergreen Currant
Symphoricarpos mollis	Creeping Snowberry
Vaccinium ovatum	Box Blueberry

Pacific Northwest (Oregon and Washington)

Botanical name	Common name
°Camellia japonica	Camellia
Enkianthus	Enkianthus
Fatshedera lizei	Fatshedera
Hydrangea anomala petiolaris	Climbing Hydrangea
Ilex aquifolium	Holly
Mahonia aquifolium	Oregon Holly Grape
Photinia frazeri	Photina
Pinus mugo	Mugho Pine
°Rhododendron	Azalea
°Rhododendron	Rhododendron
Sarcococca hookeriana humilis	Small Himalayan Sarcococca

GROUND COVERS

East (New York City and Long Island, south to Maryland)

Botanical name	Common name
Aegpodium podograria	Goutweed
Ajuga reptans	Bugle
Akebia quinata	Five-leaf Akebia
Ampelopsis brevipedunculata	Porcelain Vine
Asperula odorata	Sweet Woodruff

° Particularly choice varieties:
　　Camellia japonica: 'Grandiflora Roses,' 'C.M. Wilson,' 'Blood of China,' 'Giulid Nuccio,' 'Finlandia,' 'Frizzle White,' 'Tinsle'
　　Azaleas, Gable and Glendale Hybrids: 'Dorothy Gish,' 'Dr. Bergman'
　　Azaleas, Gumpo Hybrids: 'Pericat,' 'Roseaflora'
　　Rhododendrons: 'Loder's White,' Loderi Hybrids (Large Plants and Flowers); 'Mrs. Betty Robertson,' Naomi Hybrids; 'Snow Lady,' 'Cilpenense,' 'Anne Bedford,' 'Bow Bells'

Botanical name	Common name
Convallaria majalis	Lily of the valley
Epimedium (Hybrids)	Epimedium
Erythronium americanum	Common Fawn Lily
Euonymus fortunei colorata	Purple Wintercreeper
Galax aphylla	Galax
Hedera canariensis "variegata"	Algerian Ivy
Hedera helix "baltica"	Baltic Ivy
Hosta (species)	Hosta or Plantain Lily
Lamium galeobdalon	Yellow Archangel
Lamium maculatum	Spotted Dead Nettle
Lysimachia nummularia	Moneywort or Creeping Charlie
Mitchella repens	Partridgeberry
Pachysandra procumbens	Allegheny Pachysandra
Pachysandra terminalis	Japanese Spurge
Sarcococca hookeriana humilis	Small Himalayan Sarcococca
Shortia galacifolia	Oconee Bells
Thymus (species)	Thyme
Tiarella cordifolia	Allegheny Foam flower
Vancouveria (species)	Barrenwort
Vinca minor	Myrtle, Periwinkle
Viola (species)	Violets
Waldsteinia fragarioides	Barren Strawberry
Xanthorhiza simplicissima	Yellowroot

New England

Botanical name	Common name
Hedera helix	English Ivy
Lysimachia nummularia	Moneywort, Creeping Charlie
Paxistima canbyi	Canby Pachistima
Pachysandra terminalis	Japanese Spurge
Polygonum reynoutria	Reynoutria Fleeceflower
Vinca minor	Periwinkle, Myrtle

Central (Illinois, Michigan, Minnesota south to Missouri, west to Colorado)

Botanical name	Common name
Ajuga reptans	Bugle
Arctostaphylos uva-ursi	Bearberry
Asarum caudatum	Wild Ginger
Asperula odorata	Sweet Woodruff
Convallaria majalis	Lily of the valley
Cotoneaster (species)	Cotoneasters
Euonymus fortunei	Wintercreeper
Euonymus fortunei coloratus	Purple Wintercreeper
Euonymus fortunei 'Tempo'	Wintercreeper
Hedera helix 'Baltica'	Baltic Ivy
Hedera helix 'Thorndale'	Thorndale Ivy
Heuchera sanguinea	Coral-bells
Hosta (species)	Hosta or Plantain Lily
Juniperus communis	Common Juniper
Lamium maculata	Spotted Dead Nettle
Liriope spicata	Creeping Lilyturf
Mahonia aquifolium	Oregon Holly Grape
Mazus reptans	Mazus
Pachysandra terminalis	Japanese Spurge
Tiarella cordifolia	Allegheny Foam Flower
Vinca minor	Periwinkle, Myrtle

South (Washington, D.C., South Carolina south to Louisiana)

Botanical name	Common name
Ajuga reptans	Bugle
Ardesia japonica	Ardesia
Convallaria Majalis	Lily of the valley
Cyperus diffusus	Flatsedge
Cyrtomium falcatum	Japanese Holly Fern
Glechoma	Ground Ivy
Hedera (species)	Ivy
Hypericum calycinum	Aaron's Beard St. Johnswort
Liriope muscari	Lilyturf
Liriope spicata	Creeping Lilyturf
Mondo japonicum	Mondo Grass
Rubus calycinoides	Creeping Blackberry
Saxifraga sarmentosa	Strawberry Geranium
Stenotaphrum secundatum	St. Augustine Grass
Trachelospermum jasminoides	Confederate Jasmine

California (San Francisco south to San Diego)

Botanical name	Common name
Ajuga reptans	Bugle
Asarum caudatum	Wild Ginger
Bergenia Stracheyi	Bergenia
Hedera helix (species)	Ivy
Helleborus (species)	Christmas and Lenten Rose
Hypericum foremosum scouleri	St. John's Wort
Liriope	Lilyturf
Ophiopogon	
Ranunculus repens	Double Creeping Buttercup
Sarcococca hookeriana humilis	Small Himalayan Sarcococca
Tolmiea menziesii	Pickaback or Piggyback
Tradescantia (species)	Wandering Jew
Vinca minor and major	Periwinkle, Myrtle

Pacific Northwest (Oregon and Washington)

Botanical name	Common name
Arabis albida	Rock Cress
Asarum caudatum	Wild Ginger
Asperula odorata	Sweet Woodruff
Hedera helix	Ivy
Myosotis sylvatica	Forget-me-not
Pachysandra terminalis	Pachysandra
Vinca minor and major	Periwinkle, Myrtle

PERENNIALS

East (New York City and Long Island, south to Maryland)

Botanical name	Common name
Actaea alba	White Baneberry
Actaea rubra	Red Baneberry
Adiantum pedatum	American Maidenhair Fern
Aegpodium Podagaria	Goutweed

Botanical name	Common name
Arisaema triphyllum	Jack-in-the-Pulpit
Asarum canadense	Wild Ginger
Asperula odorata	Sweet Woodruff
Asplenium (species)	Spleenworts
Astilbe (species)	Astilbes
Athyrium filix-femina	Lady Fern
Begonia evansiana	Hardy Begonia
Bergenia cordifolia	Heartleaf Bergenia
Chimaphila maculata	Striped Pipsissewa
Cimicifuga racemosa	Snakeroot
Convallaria majalis	Lily of the valley
Cyclamen neapolitanicum	Hardy Cyclamen
Cypripedium acaule	Lady's-slipper
Dicentra exima	Fringed Bleeding Heart
Dicentra spectabilis	Common Bleeding Heart
Digitalis (hybrids) (biennial)	Foxglove
Dryopteris (species)	Ferns
Filipendula hexapetala	Double Dropwort
Fuchsia (hardy)	Fuchsias
Gentiana septemfida	Gentian
Hosta (species)	Plantain Lily
Helleborus	Hellebores and Roses
Heuchera sanguinea	Coral-bells
Liriope muscari	Lilyturf
Macleaya cordata	Plume Poppy
Mazus reptans	Mazus
Mertensia virginica	Virginia Bluebells
Mitchella repens	Partridgeberry
Myosotis (biennial)	Forget-me-not
Osmunda claytoniana	Interrupted Fern
Podophyllum peltatum	May Apple
Polystichum acrostichoides	Christmas Fern

New England

Botanical name	Common name
Aegpodium podagaria	Goutweed
Ajuga	Bugle
Anemones (species)	Anemones
Astilbe	Astilbes
Convallaria majalis	Lily of the valley
Dicentra (species)	Bleeding Heart
	Ferns (varieties)
Hosta (species)	Hosta or Plantain Lily
Mertensia virginica	Virginia Bluebells
Primula (species)	Primroses
Platycodon grandiflorum	Balloonflower
Viola	Violet

Central (Illinois, Michigan, Minnesota south to Missouri, west to Colorado)

Botanical name	Common name
Actaea alba	White Baneberry
Actaea rubra	Red Baneberry
Adiantum pedatum	Maidenhair Fern
Aepodium podagaria	Goutweed

Botanical name	Common name
Aquilegia (species and cultivars)	Columbines
Asarum canadense	Wild Ginger
Asarum europaeum	European Wild Ginger
Asperula odorata	Sweet Woodruff
Astilbe (species)	Astilbes
Cimicifuga racemosa	Snakeroot
Cypripedium	Ladys-slippers
Dicentra exima	Fringed Bleedingheart
Dicentra spectabilis	Bleeding Heart
Dictamnus albus	Gasplant
Epimedium	Barrenwort
Hemerocallis (species)	Daylily
Hesperis matronalis	Sweet Rocket
Hosta (species)	Plantain Lily
Lamium	Dead Nettle
Phlox divaricata	Wild Blue Phlox
Polemonium	Jacob's Ladder
Polystichum acrostichoides	Christmas Fern
Sanguinaria canadensis	Bloodroot
Tiarella cordifolia	Foam Flower

South (Washington, D.C., South Carolina south to Louisiana)

Botanical name	Common name
Aconitum	Monkshood
Aspidistra elatior	Cast-iron Plant
Astilbe	Astilbe
Athyrium asplenioides	Lady Fern
Bergenia	Bergenia
Cimicifuga racemosa	Snakeroot
Doronicum	Leopard's-bane
Dryopteris ludoviciana	Florida Shield Fern
Helleborus	Christmas Rose
Hosta (species)	Plantain Lily
Onoclea sensibilis	Sensitive Fern
Viola (species)	Violets

California (San Francisco south to San Diego)

Botanical name	Common name
Adiantum Capillus-veneris	Venus-hair Fern
Ajuga reptans	Bugle
Anthemis nobilis	
Aspidistra elatior	Cast-iron Plant
Bergenia cordifolia	Bergenia
Chlorophytum elatum	Spider Plant
Clivia (species)	Clivia
Cyclamen indicum	Cyclamen
Fragaria californica	Strawberry Wood
Heuchera maxima	Alumroot
Juncus patens	Wire Grass
Lilium 'Bellingham Hybrids'	Lily
L. humboldti	Humboldt Lily
L. pardalinum	Leopard Lily
L. wardii	Ward Lily
Lobelia cardinalis	Cardinal Flower
Polypodium scouleri	Leatherleaf Fern

Pacific Northwest (Oregon and Washington)

Botanical name	Common name
Anemone blanda	Anemone
Astilbe	Astilbe or Spirea
Aquilegia	Columbine
Campanula persicifolia	Peach-leaved Bellflower
Dicentra formosa	Dwarf Western Bleeding Heart
Dodecatheon	Shooting Star
Erythronium	Trout Lily, Lamb's Tongue
Ferns (species)	Ferns
Fuchsia	Fuchsia
Helleborus niger	Christmas Rose
Hosta	Hosta or Plantain Lily
Primula polyantha	Primrose
Trillium	Wake Robin
Viola cornuta, V. odorata	Violets

ANNUALS

East (New York City and Long Island, south to Maryland)

Botanical name	Common name
Ageratum houstonianum	Ageratum
Begonia semperflorens	Wax Begonias
Begonia tuberosa	Tuberous Begonia
Bellis perennis	English Daisy
Browallia	Browallia
Caladium	Caladium
Campanula	Bellflower
Convallaria majalis	Lily of the valley
Celosia argentea	Feather Cockscomb
Coleus	Coleus
Fuchsia (hybrids)	Fuchsia
Iberis (species)	Candytuft
Impatiens, balsamina, biflora, sultanii	Patience Plant
Lobelia erinus	Edging Lobelia
Lobularia maritima	Sweet Alyssum
Myosotis sylvatica	Woodland Forget-me-not
Nicotiana	Tobacco Plant
Torenia fournieri	Blue Torenia
Vinca	Myrtle

New England

Botanical name	Common name
Myosotis sylvatica (biennial)	Woodland Forget-me-not
Digitalis (biennial)	Foxglove

Central (Illinois, Michigan, Minnesota south to Missouri, west to Colorado)

Botanical name	Common name
Ageratum houstonianum	Ageratum
Begonia semperflorens	Wax Begonia
Caladium	Caladium
Clarkia	Clarkia
Coleus (species)	Coleus

Botanical name	Common name
Digitalis purpurea (biennial)	Foxglove
Godetia	Godetia
Impatiens balsamina, I. sultani	Patience Plant
Lobelia erinus	Lobelia
Myosotis sylvatica	Woodland Forget-me-not
Nicotiana alata	Winged Tobacco
Vinca rosea	Myrtle
Viola (species)	Violets

South (Washington, D.C., South Carolina south to Louisiana)

Botanical name	Common name
Achimenes	Achimenes
Begonia semperflorens	Wax Begonia
Caladium bicolor	Caladium
Coleus	Coleus
Impatiens balsamina, I. sultani	Patience Plant
Myosotis sylvatica	Woodland Forget-me-not
Viola	Violets

California (San Francisco south to San Diego)

Botanical name	Common name
Bellis perennis	English Daisy
Cinerraria	Cinerraria
Claytonia	Spring Beauty
Collins bicolor	Chinese Houses
Impatiens (species)	Patience Plant
Martricaria	Matricaria
Mimulus	Monkey Flower
Oenothera (species)	
Oxalis	Wood Sorrel
Tropaeolum majus	Nasturtium

Pacific Northwest (Oregon and Washington)

Botanical name	Common name
Alocasia	Alocasia
Begonia semperflorens	Wax Begonia
Begonia tuberosa	Tuberous Begonia
Caladium bicolor	Caladium
Coleus blumei	Coleus
Fritillaria meleagris	Checkered Lily
Impatiens roylei	Touch-me-not
Ricinus	Castor Bean
Vinca rosea	Periwinkle
Viola tricolor hortensis	Pansy

APPENDIX 3

❖❖❖❖❖❖❖❖❖❖❖

Where to Buy
Shade-loving Plants

These lists were mainly provided
by each plant society

AZALEAS, RHODODENDRONS

Avalon Mountain Gardens, Dana, North Carolina 28724
Warren Bardsiefen, Box 88, Bellvale, New York 10902
Carolson's Gardens, Box 305, South Salem, New York 10590
J. Harold Clarke, Long Beach, Washington 98631
Comerford's, Box 100, Marion, Oregon 97359
Cranguyma Farms Nursery, Long Beach, Washington 98631
Bill Dodd Nurseries, Box 235, Semmes, Alabama 36575
Gossler Farms Nursery, 1200 Weaver Road, Springfield, Oregon 97477
Greer Gardens, 1280 Goodpasture Island Road, Eugene, Oregon 97401
Hall Nursery, 135 Norten Park, Bridgewater, Maine 02324
Thomas Henry Nursery, 7811 Stratford Drive N.E., Brooks, Oregon 97305
Island Gardens, 701 Goodpasture Island Road, Eugene, Oregon 97401
LaBars' Rhododendron Nursery, Box 111, Stroudsburg, Pennsylvania 18360
H.L. Larson, 3656 Bridgeport Way, Tacoma, Washington 98466
Nuccio's Nurseries, 3555 Chadney Trail, Altadena, California 91001
Orchard Nursery, Box 7224, Mobile, Alabama 36607
Orinda Nursery, Bridgeville, Delaware 19933
Rainier Mt. Alpine Gardens, 2007 S. 126th Street, Seattle, Washington 98168
G.C. Robinson Nursery, 56 N. Georgia Avenue, Mobile, Alabama 36604
A. Shammarello and Son Nursery, 4508 Monticello Blvd.; South Euclid, Ohio 44143
The Tingle Nursery, Pittsville, Maryland 21850
White Flower Farm, Litchfield, Connecticut 06759

CAMELLIAS

Redwood Empire Camellias, 7949 Lynch Road, Sebastopol, California 95472
Stewart's Camellia Nursery, 2403 Bonaventure Road, Savannah, Georgia 31404
Tammia Nursery, P.O. Box 157, Slidell, Louisiana 70458
Wilkes Nursery, Rt. 6, Moultrie, Georgia 31768

Camellia cuttings for grafting and propagating
Beard's Nursery, Rt. 6, Moultrie, Georgia 31768
Mark S. Cannon, 300 Montezuma Avenue, Dothan, Alabama 36301
Bell Fontaine Nursery, Rt. 3, Box 546, Mobile, Alabama 36582
Ray Gentry, P.O. Box 6626, Jackson, Mississippi 39212
Peach County Nursery, Box 136-C, Route 3, Fort Valley, Georgia 31030

DAYLILIES

J. Herbert Alexander, Middleboro, Massachusetts 02346
Blackburn's Olinda Gardens, R. 4, Box 441, Rocky Mount, North Carolina 27801
Jack Caldwell, Box 39051, Birmingham, Alabama 35208
Frank Child's Nursery, Jenkinsburg, Georgia 30234
Davidson Gardens, 1215 Church Street, Decatur, Georgia 30030
Englerth Gardens, Rt. 1, Hopkins, Minnesota 49328
The Hancock Gardens, 210 2nd Avenue S.E., Steele, North Dakota 58482
Howard J. Hite, 270 Waddington Road, Birmingham, Michigan 48009
Howell Gardens, Letitia Street, Baton Rouge, Louisiana 70808
Hughes Garden, Rt. 3, Box 127, Mansfield, Texas 76063
Iron Gate Gardens, Rt. 3, Box 101, Kings Mountain, North Carolina 28086
Lemington Gardens, 7007 Manchester Avenue, Kansas City, Missouri 64133
Louisiana Nursery, Rt. 1, Box 43, Opelousas, Louisiana 70570
Maxwell's Garden, Rt. 1, Box 155, Olla, Louisiana 71465
Parry Nurseries, Signal Mountain, Tennessee 37377
C.G. Simon Nursery, Box 2873, Lafayette, Louisiana 70501
Starmont Daylily Farm, 16415 Shady Grove Road, Gaithersburg, Maryland 20760
Tanner's Garden, Box 385, Chenneyville, Louisiana 71325
Tranquil Lake Nursery, 45 River Street, Rehoboth, Maine 02769
Wheeler's Daylily Farm, 10024 Shady Lane, Houston, Texas 77016
Gilbert H. Wild and Son, Sarcoxie, Missouri 64862
Garden of Aden, 980 Stanton Avenue, Baldwin, New York 11510

GROUND COVERS

Brimfield Gardens Nursery, 245 Brimfield Road, Wethersfield, Connecticut 06109
The Rock Garden, Litchfield, Maine 04350
Mayfair Nurseries, Nichols, New York 13812
Oak Park Nurseries, East Patchogue, New York 11772
Sterns Nurseries, Geneva, New York 14456
E.C. Robbins, Ashford, McDowell County, North Carolina 28603
Wayside Gardens, Hodges, South Carolina 29695
Rocknoll Nursery, Morrow, Ohio 45152
Spring Hill Nurseries, 311 Elm Street, Tipp City, Ohio 45371
OsBow Botanical Gardens, Gresham, Oregon 97030
Cark Starker Gardens, Jennings Lodge, Oregon 97267
Charles Thurman, Rt. 2, Box 259, Spokane, Washington 99207

HOLLY

°American Holly Products, Inc., P.O. Box 754, Millville, New Jersey 08332
Bosley Nurseries, 9579 Mentor Avenue, Mentor, Ohio 44060
°Brownell Farms, Box 22025, Milwaukie, Oregon 97222
Busch Nurseries, Inc., 7903 Thompson Run Road, Pittsburgh, Pennsylvania 15237
Cartwright Nurseries, Collierville, Tennessee 38017
Tom Dilatush, R.R. 4, Robbinsville, New Jersey 08691
Tom Dodd Nurseries, P.O. Box 35, Semmes, Alabama 36575
Grandview Nurseries, R.F.D. Box 54, Youngsville, Louisiana 70592
Gulf Stream Nurseries, Inc., Wachapreague, Virginia 23480
Calvin Harman, Stoval, Georgia 32082
Holly Hill Farms, B.H. Brockley & Co., Earlville, Maryland 21919
Houlihan Nursery Co., 640 N. Mosley Road, Creve Coeur, Missouri 63141
Kalmia Farms, Tridelphia Road, Clarksville, Maryland 21029
Kingsville Nurseries, Kingsville, Maryland 21087
°McLean Holly Nursery, 9010 Satyr Hill Road, Baltimore, Maryland 21234
Orlando S. Pride, 523 Fifth Street, Butler, Pennsylvania 16001
Robins Nurseries, Willard, North Carolina 28478
°Simpson Orchard Company Inc., 1504 Wheatland Road, Vincinnes, Indiana 47591
Star Roses, West Grove, Pennsylvania 19390
Steeds' Nursery, Candor, North Carolina 27229
°Tingle Nursery Co., Pittsville, Maryland 21850
°Alfred Teufel Nursery, 12345 N.W. Barnes Road, Portland, Oregon 97229
°John Vermeulen & Son, Inc., Box 267 N. Woodfern Road, Neshanic Station, New
    Jersey 08853
Watnong Nurseries, Morris Plains, New Jersey 07950
°John Wieman Holly, 10819 S.W. Capitol Highway, Portland, Oregon 97219
Wright Nurseries, P.O. Box 390, Cairo, Georgia 31728

HOSTAS

Minks Fairway Gardens, 114 The Fairway, Albert Lea, Minnesota 46007
Savory's Greenhouses, 5300 Whiting Avenue, Minneapolis, Minnesota 55435
Alex J. Summers, Willets Road W., Roslyn, New York 11576
Wayside Gardens, Hodges, South Carolina 29695
Garden of Aden, 980 Stanton Avenue, Baldwin, New York 11510

IVY

Cherry Lane Nurseries, La Plata, Maryland 20646
Merry Gardens, Camden, Maine 04843
The Garden Spot, Rosewood Drive, Columbia, South Carolina 29205

PRIMROSES

Far North Gardens, 15621 Auburndale Avenue, Livonia, Michigan 48154
Skyhook Farm, Johnson, Vermont 05656

WILD FLOWERS AND FERNS

Alpenglow Gardens, 13328 King George Highway, Surrey, B.C. V3T 2T6, Canada
Alpines West Nursery, Rt. 2, Box 259, Spokane, Washington 99207

° Will mail small plants up to one foot in height.

Edelweiss Gardens, 54 Robbinsville-Allentown Road, P.O. Box 66R, Robbinsville, New Jersey 08691
Ferndale Nursery and Greenhouse, P.O. Box 218, Askov, Minnesota 55704
Green Bush Gardens, Charlotte, Vermont 05445
Gardens of the Blue Ridge, Ashford, McDowell County, North Carolina 28603
Ruth Hardy's Red Cedar Wildflower Nursery, Falls Village, Connecticut 06031
Leatherman's Gardens, 2637 N. Lee Avenue, South El Monte, California 91733
Lounsberry Gardens, P.O. Box 135, Oakford, Illinois 62673
Mincemoyers, R.D. 5, Box 379, Jackson, New Jersey 08527
Orchid Gardens, Route 1, Box 245, Grand Rapids, Minnesota 55744
Putney Nursery, Putney, Vermont 05346
Savage Wildflower Gardens, P.O. 163, McMinnville, Tennessee 37110
Sperka's Woodland Acres Nursery, Rt. 2, Crivitz, Wisconsin 54114
The Three Laurels, Route 3, Box 15, Marshall, North Carolina 28753
The Wild Garden, 8423 N.E. 119th, Kirkland, Washington 98033

WILD FLOWER SEEDS and FERN SPORES

Leslie's Wild Flower Nursery, 30 Summer Street, Methuen, Massachusetts 01844
Clyde Robin Seed Company Inc., P.O. Box 2855, Castro Valley, California 94546
Harry E. Saier, Dimondale, Michigan 48821

APPENDIX 4

✿❀✿❀✿❀✿❀✿❀✿❀✿

Specialized Plant Societies

American Begonia Society, Inc.
Mrs. Jacqueline Garinger
6333 W. 85th Place
Los Angeles, California 90045
$4 yearly

American Camellia Society
Milton H. Brown
P.O. Box 212
Fort Valley, Georgia 31030
$7.50 yearly

The American Fern Society
Terry R. Webster
Biological Sciences Group
University of Connecticut
Storrs, Connecticut 06268
$5 yearly

American Hemerocallis Society
Mrs. Arthur W. Parry
Signal Mountain, Tennessee 37377
$7.50 yearly

American Hosta Society
Mrs. Nancy Minks
114 The Fairway
Albert Lea, Minnesota 56007
$5 yearly

American Ivy Society
National Center for American
    Horticulture
Mount Vernon, Virginia 22121
$7.50 yearly

American Primose Society
Mrs. Thelma Genheimer
7100 N.E. 78th Avenue
Portland, Oregon 97213
$5 yearly

American Rhododendron Society
2232 N.E. 78th Avenue
Portland, Oregon 97213
$12 yearly

American Rock Garden Society
Milton S. Mulloy
90 Pierpont Road
Waterbury, Connecticut 06705
$5 yearly

California Native Plant Society
Joyce E. Burr
2380 Ellsworth Street
Berkeley, California 94704
$8 yearly

Holly Society of America, Inc.
Mr. Bluett C. Green, Jr.
407 Fountain Green Road
Bel Air, Maryland 21014
$5 yearly

Los Angeles International Fern Society
Wilbur W. Olson
2423 Burritt Avenue
Redondo Beach, California 90278
$4.50 yearly

APPENDIX 5

✿╳✿╳✿╳✿╳✿╳✿╳✿

Miscellaneous Suppliers

Fiberglass, plastic pools, pumps etc.
William Tricker, Inc.
174 Allendale Ave.
Saddle River, New Jersey 07458

and also at
7125 Tanglewood Drive
Independence, Ohio 44131

Index

Achimenes (*Achimenes*), 175, 176
Acidity, litmus test for, 16, 19
  described, 29
Aconite (*Eranthis*), 180–81
Agriculture, U.S. Department of, 130
Ajuga, 118–19
Akebia, 116–17
Alabama Fothergilla (*Fothergilla monticola, Fothergilla gardenii*),
  129, 131
Aluminum sulphate, 29
American Camellia Society, 146
American Hemerocallis Society, 81
American Hosta Society, 124
American Ivy Society, 109
American Primrose Society, 89
American Rhododendron Society, 156,
  160
Ammonium phosphate, 70
Ammonium sulphate, 16, 19, 70
Andromeda (*Pieris japonica*), 129,
  143–44
Anemones, 90–91
Arnold Arboretum, 135
Arrowwood Viburnum (*Viburnum dentatum*), 162–63
Ash trees, 70
Asparagus Fern, 72
Asters, 86–87
Astilbe (*Astilbe*), 73–74
Autumn Aconite (*Aconitum fishcheri, Aconitum wilsonii*), 86
Azaleas, 129, 155–60

Ballard, Ernest, 86

Balloonflower (*Platycodon grandiforum*), 77
Baneberry (*Actaea pachypoda, Actaea rubra*), 30–31
Barberry (*Berberis thunbergii, Berberis verruculosa*), 144–45
Barren Strawberry (*Waldstenia fragarioides*), 116
Barrenwort (*Epimedium*), 117–18
Bayberry (*Myrica penyslvanica*), 131–32
Beard Tongue (*Pentstemon*), 91–92
Beech trees, 16
Bergenia (*Bergenia cordifolia*), 74
Berger, Karl August von, 74
Bird's-nest Fern (*Asplenium*), 72
Bishop's-Cap (*Mitella diphylla*), 17, 31
Bishop's-Hat (*Epimedium*), 117–18
Bittersweet (*Celastrus scandens, Celastrus losneri*), 166–67
Black Haw (*Viburnum prunifolium*),
  163–64
Black Snakeroot (*Cimicifuga racemosa*), 34–35
Bleeding Heart (*Dicentra*), 75
Bloodroot (*Sanguinaria canadensis*),
  21, 33
Bluebeads (*Clintonia borealis*), 51
Blue Cohosh (*Caulophyllum thalictroides*), 34
Bogs/bog garden, 16, 20–21
  plants to grow in, 51–53
Boston Ivy (*Parthenocissus tricuspidata*), 167–68
Broad Beech Fern (*Thelypteris hexagonoptera*), 60

Browallia (*Browallia speciosa major*), 92–93
Bugbane (*Cimicifuga racemosa*), 34–35
Bugle (*Ajuga reptans*), 118–19
Bulblet Bladder Fern (*Cystopteris bulbifera*), 63
Bulbs, 23
    hardy, 175, 180–93
    light conditions required by, 174–75
    planting instructions on, 175
    tender, 175–80
    see also individual names of
Bush-Brown, James, 149
Bush Honeysuckle (*Diervilla sessilifolia*), 132–33
Buttercups, 19
Butterfly Flower (*Schizanthus pinnatus*), 93

Caladium, 175, 177–78
Camassia, 181
Camellia (*Camellia japonica, Camellia sasanqua, Camellia reticulata*), 145–47
Canada Mayflower (*Maianthemum canadense*), 36
Canada Violet (*Viola canadensis*), 48
Candytuft (*Iberis sempervirens*), 75–76
Cardinal Flower (*Lobelia cardinalis, Lobelia siphilitica*), 70, 76–77
Chinese Bellflower (*Platycodon grandiforum*), 77
Chinese Bittersweet (*Celastrus losneri*), 167
Chlorophyll, 12
Christmas Fern (*Polystichum acrostichoides*), 57–58
Christmas Rose (*Helleborus niger*), 78–79
Cinnamon Fern (*Osmunda cinnamomea*), 61–62
Clay, 14
Clethra, 129
Climbing Hydrangea (*Hydrangea petiolaris*), 168–69
Cohosh (*Cimicifuga racemosa*), 34–35
Coleus, 94–95
Columbine (*Aquilegia caerulea, Aquilegia canadensis*), 79–80

Common Maidenhair (*Adiantum pedatum*), 65
Common Polypody (*Polypodium vulgare*), 58
Compost, 13, 16
    manufacture of, 25–28
    see also Humus
Corms, 23
Cottonseed meal, 16, 19
Cowberry (*Vaccinium vitis-idaea*), 105
Creeping Snowberry (*Gaultheria hispidula*), 53
Creeping Thyme (*Thymus serpyllum*), 103, 105–6
Crested Iris (*Iris cristata*), 119–20
Crested Shield Fern (*Dryopteris cristata*), 63
Crocus, 182–83
Cutleaf Stephanandra (*Stephanandra incisa*), 133
Cyclamen, 183–84

Daffodils (*Narcissus*), 184
Day Lily (*Hemerocallis*), 80–81
Dietz, Marjorie J., 135
Dioscorides, 117
Dog Violet (*Viola conspersa*), 49
Drooping Leucothoë (*Leucothoë Caetsbaei*), 106–7, 147
Dutch Crocus, 182–83
Dutchman's-Breeches (*Dicentra cucullaria*), 21, 32, 35–36
Dutchman's-Pipe (*Aristolochia durior*), 169
Dwarf Trillium (*T. nivale*), 46

Earthworms, 19, 27–28
Ebony Spleenwort (*Asplenium platyneuron*), 59–60
Elephant's Ear (*Colocasia antiquorum*), 175, 178–79
Elm trees, 16, 70
English Bluebells (*Scilla nonscripta*), 181
English Yew (*Taxus baccata*), 164
Epimedium, 117–18
Euonymus (*Euonymus fortunei, Euonymus fortunei coloratus*), 107–8
Evergreens, 30
    ground covering plants, 104, 105–15

shrubs, 143–65
woodland plants, 53–56, 57–60
see also individual names of

Fairy Bell (*Disporum*), 81
False Lily of the Valley (*Maianthemum canadense*), 36
False Solomon's-seal (*Smilactina racemosa*), 37
False Spirea (*Sorbaria sorbifolia*), 133–34
Ferns, 22, 56–68
evergreen, 30, 57–60
indoor, 72
see also individual names of
Ferrand, Beatrix, 135
Fertilizers, 28, 157
see also Compost
Five-leaf Akebia (*Akebia quinata*), 116–17
Five-leaf Aralia (*Acanthopanax sieboldianus*), 134
Flowering plants
annuals, 71–72, 92–101
light conditions required by, 69–70
perennials, 71, 72–91
soil, preparation of for, 70, 73
see also individual names of
Foam Flower (*Tiarella cordifolia*), 24, 38
Forsythia, 135–36
Foxglove (*Digitalis*), 82–83
Fringed Bleeding Heart (*Dicentra eximia*), 32
Fringe tree (*Chionanthus virginicus*), 129, 136
Fuchsia (*Fuchsia magellanica*), 83–84
Funkia, 122–24

Galax (*Galax aphylla*), 54, 120
Gardener's-garters (*Phalaris arundinacea picta*), 125–26
Gentians (*Gentiana acaulis, Gentiana andrewsii*), 84
Gentius (King of Illyria), 84
Geraniums, wild, 19–20, 49–50
Gesnerias, 71
Glory-of-the-Snow (*Chionodaxa*), 185–86

Glossy Abelia (*Abelia grandifora*), 147–48
Gloxinias, 71
Goldie, John, 62
Goldie's Fern (*Dryopteris goldiana*), 62
Goutweed (*Aegopodium podagraria*), 120–21
Grape Hyacinth (*Muscari*), 186
Gravel, 17
Ground covering plants, 102–4
evergreen, 104, 105–15
herbaceous, 104, 106–27
soil, preparation of for, 104
see also individual names of
Ground Hemlock (*Taxus canadesis*), 165
Ground Ivy (*Nepeta hederacea*), 121–22
G. W. Park Seed Company, 96

Hall's Honeysuckle (*Lonicera japonica halliana*), 170
Hardiness, 130
Hay-scented Fern (*Dennstaedita punctilobula*), 60–61
Heavenly Bamboo (*Nandina domestica*), 149
Hepatica (*Heptica acutiloba, Heptica americana*), 21, 38–39
Higgins, Joseph, 97
Holly (*Ilex crenata, Ilex glabra, Ilex verticillata*), 150–51
Holly Fern (*Cyrtomium*), 72
Holly Society of America, Inc., 151
Honeysuckle (*Lonicera japonica halliana, Lonicera sempervirens, Lonicera henryi*), 170
Hooker, Sir Joseph, 158
Horse chestnut trees, 16
Hosta, 17, 103, 122–24
Humus, 13–15
acid, 19
bog gardens and, 20–21
see also Compost
Hyacinth (*Hyacinthus*), 186–87
Hydrangea, 138

Impatiens (*Impatiens balsamina, Impatiens sultanii*), 95–99

Indian Cucumber Root (*Medeola virginiana*), 51–52
Inkberry (*Ilex glabra*), 150
Insecticides, 108, 125
Intermediate Shield Fern (*Dryopteris intermedia*), 64
Interrupted Fern (*Osmunda claytoniana*), 66–67
Iris Cristata, 40
Ivy (*Hedera helix, Hedera canariensis*), 18–19, 102, 103, 108–9
Ivy Book, The Growing and Care of Ivy and Ivy Topiary, The, 102, 108

Jack-in-the-pulpit (*Arisaema triphyllum*), 23, 40–41
James I (of England), 76
Japanese Andromeda (*Pieris japonica*), 143–44
Japanese Aucuba (*Aucuba japonica*), 151
Japanese Holly (*Ilex crenata*), 150
Japanese Painted Fern (*Athyrium goeringianum*), 64
Japanese Pittosporum (*Pittosporum tobria*), 153–54
Japanese Spurge (*Pachysandra terminalis*), 110–11
Japanese Yew (*Taxus cuspidata*), 164
Jetbead (*Rhodotypos scandens*), 137

Kalm, Peter, 153
Kerria (*Kerria japonica*), 129, 137
Korean Abelia-leaf (*Abeliophyllum distichum*), 137–38

Lady Fern (*Athyrium filix-femina*), 65
Lady's-slipper (*Cypripedium acaule*), 21, 41–42
Lamium, 126
Leaf mold, 13
    oak leaf, 16, 19
    pine needle, 19
Leatherleaf Mahonia (*Mahonia bealii*), 152
Lee, George S., Jr., 184
Lenten Rose (*Helleborus orientalis*), 79
Leopard's-bane (*Doronicum plantagineum*), 85–86

Leucothoë, 129, 147
Light
    flowering plants and, 69–70
    types of, 12
Lily of the Valley (*Convallaria majalis*), 124–25
Lilyturf (*Liriope muscari*), 125
Lime, 29
Linnaeus, Carolus, 117
Lobel, Matthias de, 76
Locust trees, 70
Long Beech Fern (*Thelypteris Phegopteris*), 61

Maidenhair Fern (*Adiantum*), 65, 72
Manure, 13
Mapleleaf Viburnum (*Viburnum acerifolium*), 162
Maple trees, 16
Marginal Shield Fern (*Dryopteris marginalis*), 60
Markers, how to make, 24–25
Marsh Fern (*Thelypteris palustris*), 67
May Apple (*Podophyllum peltatum*), 23, 42–43
Meadow Blue Violet (*Viola papilionaceae*), 49
Miterwort (*Mitella diphylla*), 31
Monkey Flower (*Mimulus*), 98–99
Monkshood (*Aconitum fischeri, Aconitum wilsonii*), 86
Moonseed (*Menispermum canadense*), 171
Moss, 16–17
    see also individual types of
Mountain Laurel (*Kalmia latifolia*), 153
Mulch/mulching, 14, 70
Myrtle (*Vinca minor*), 111–12

Nandina, 149
Nannyberry (*Viburnum lentago*), 163
Narrow-leaved Chain Fern (*Woodwardia areolata*), 67
Nepeta, 103
Nephthytis, 72
New Guinea Impatiens, 97–99
New York Aster (*Aster novi-belgi*), 86

New York Fern, 31
Nurseries, 21

Oakleaf Hydrangea (*Hydrangea quercifolia*), 138
Oak trees, 16, 19, 70
Oconee Bells (*Shortia galacifolia*), 21, 23, 54–55
Oregon Holly Grape (*Mahonia aquifolium, Mahonia repens*), 112–14
Organic gardening, 25–26ff.
Ostrich Fern (*Matteuccia struthiopteris pensylvanica*), 63

Pachistima (*Paxistima canbyi*), 103, 113–14
Pachysandra, 103, 110–11
Painted Trillium (*T. undulatum*), 46
Pansies, 19
Partridgeberry (*Mitchella repens*), 55
Peat/peat moss, 13, 14, 16, 19
Pentstemon, 91–92
Periwinkle (*Vinca minor*), 103, 111–12
Perlite, 14
Philodendron, 72
Pittosporum, 153–54
Plantain Lily, 122–24
Planting beds, raised, 14
Plants
    annuals, 71–72, 91–101
    biennial, 73
    herbaceous, 72
    perennials, 71, 72–91
    see also Bulbs; Flowering plants;
        Ground Covering plants; Woodland plants
Poison Ivy, 173
Porcelain Vine (*Ampelopsis brevipedunculata*), 171
Pothos, 72
Powdered sulphur, 16, 19, 29
Primrose (*Primula*), 21, 70, 87–89
Privet (*Ligustrum*), 154
Pruning, 15, 69–70
Purple Trillium (*T. erectum*), 46

Red Chokeberry (*Aronia arbutifolia*), 139
Rhizomes, 23

Rhododendrons, 129, 155–60
Ribbon Grass (*Phalaris arundinacea picta*), 125–26
Rodale, J. I., 26
Roots
    clustered and fibrous, 23
    of trees, 15–17
Rothchild, Lord Lionel, 158, 159
Royal Fern (*Osmunda regalis spectabilis*), 67–68
Runners, 24

Salal (*Gaultheria shallon*), 160–61
Salvia (*Salvia*), 99–100
Sand, 14
Scarlet Sage (*Salvia*), 99–100
Seaweed, 14
Seeds, 21
Selecting Shrubs for Shady Areas, 130
Shooting Star (*Dodecatheon Meadia*), 89
Showy Orchis (*Orchis spectabilis*), 21, 43
Shrubs, 106–7, 128–29
    deciduous, 131–43
    evergreen, 143–65
    selection and care of, 130
    soil, preparation of for, 129
    see also individual names of
Shrubs and Trees for the Home Landscape, 149
Sinningias, 71
Skimmia (*Skimmia japonica*), 129, 161
Skunk Cabbage (*Symplocarpus foetidus*), 52–53
Small Himalayan Sarcococca (*Sarcococca hookeriana humilis*), 114–15
Snowberry (*Symphoricarpos albus*), 140
Snowdrops (*Galanthus*), 187–88
Snowflake (*Leucojum*), 188–89
Snow Trillium (*T. grandiflorum*), 46
Soil
    acid, 16, 19, 28, 70
        test for, 29
    alkaline, 28, 29, 70
    boggy, 15–16, 20–21
    clay, 14

Soil (*continued*)
  preparation of, 13–15
    flowering plants, 70
    ground covering plants, 104
    shrubs, 129
    woodland plants, 19, 29
  sandy, 14
  water, retention of by, 14
Solomon's Seal (*Polygonatum bi-florum*), 23, 44
Spathiphyllum, 72
Sphagnum Moss, 20–21
Spicebush (*Lindera benzoin*), 140
Spider mites, 125
Spinulose Shield Fern (*Dryopteris spinulosa*), 66
Spirea, 73
Spotted Dead Nettle (*Lamium maculatum*), 126
Squills (*Scilla hispanica, Scilla sibirica, Scilla nonscripta*), 181
Star-of-bethlehem (*Ornithogalum*), 189
Stephanandra, 133
Stephanotis, 72
Stinking Benjamin, 46
Stolons, 110–11
Stonecrop (*Sedum acre, Sedum album*), 115
Striped Squill (*Puschkinia scilloides*), 190
Summer Sweet (*Clethra alnifolia*), 141
Superphosphate, 16, 19
Sweet Pepper Bush (*Clethra alnifolia*), 141
Sweet Potato (*Impomoea batatus*), 172–73
Sweet White Violet (*Viola blanda*), 48–49
Sweet Woodruff (*Asperulo odorata*), 127

Taro Root (*Colocasia esculenta*), 179
Totemeir, Carl, 83–84
Trees, 11
  pruning of, 15, 69–70
  roots, 15–17
  see also individual names of
Trillium (*T. grandiflorum, T. ovatum, T. erectum, T. nivale, T. rivale, T. undulatum*), 23, 45–46

Trout Lilies (*Erythronium*), 190
Trumpet Honeysuckle (*Lonicera sempervirens*), 170
Tuberous Begonias, 175, 179–80
Tulips (*Tulipa*), 191–93

Urea, 70

Viburnum, 162–64
Vines, 24, 166–73
  see also individual names of
Violets (*Viola canadensis, V. pubescens, V. blanda, V. papilonacea, V. conspersa*), 19, 20, 21, 23, 47–49
Virginia Bluebells (*Mertensia virginica*), 46–47
Virginia Chain Fern (*Woodwardia virginica*), 68
Virginia Creeper (*Parthenocissus quinquefolia*), 173

Waterer, Anthony, 159
Wax Begonia (*Begonia semperforens*), 100–101
Western Snow Trillium (*T. rivale*), 46
White Forsythia, 137–38
White Trillium (*T. grandiflorum*), 46
Wildflowers, 21, 22–23, 29–50
  see also individual names of
Wild Geranium (*Geranium maculatum*), 19–20, 49–50
Wild Ginger (*Asarum canadense*), 50
Willow trees, 14–15
Windflower (*Anemone japonica, Anemone vitifolia*), 90–91
Winterberry (*Ilex verticillata*), 150
Wintercreeper (*Euonymus fortunei, Euonymus fortunei coloratus*), 107–8
Wintergreen (*Gaultheria procumbens*), 55–56
Winter Hazel (*Corylopsis spicata, Corylopsis paucifora, Corylopsis sinesis*), 142
Winters, Harold, 97
Wishbone Flower (*Torenia*), 101
Witch Hazel (*Hamamelis virginiana*), 142–43

Witherod (*Viburnum cassinoidea*), 162
Wood Hyacinths (*Scilla hispanica*), 181
Woodland plants/garden, 18–19, 89
  bogs, natural or artificial, 20–21
    plants to grow in, 51–53
  collection of plants, 21–23
  compost, manufacture of for, 25–28
  evergreen plants, 53–56, 57–60
  ferns, 56–68
  growth, encouragement of, 23–24

  maintenance of, 19–20
  marking site of plants, 24–25
  soil, preparation of for, 19, 29
  wildflowers, list of, 29–50
  see also individual names of plants

Yellowroot (*Xanthorhiza simplicissima*),
  127
Yew (*Taxus cuspidata, Taxus baccata,
  Taxus media*), 164–65